C000180258

Prisons
EXPOSED

Prisons
EXPOSED

Michael O'Brien

yLolfa

First impression: 2012

© Copyright Michael O'Brien and Y Lolfa Cyf., 2012

The contents of this book are subject to copyright, and may
not be reproduced by any means, mechanical or electronic,
without the prior, written consent of the publishers.

Cover design: Y Lolfa

ISBN: 978 184771 4114

Published and printed in Wales
on paper from well maintained forests
by Y Lolfa Cyf., Talybont, Ceredigion SY24 5HE
website www.ylolfa.com
e-mail ylolfa@ylolfa.com
tel 01970 832 304
fax 832 782

CONTENTS

In loving memory of our son

Dylan Michael James O'Brien

04/02/2010 – 15/06/2012

Our precious little angel, the biggest star in the sky.

R.I.P.

INTRODUCTION

PRISON SERVICE POLICY dictates that all prisoners will be treated with humanity and dignity while in their care. Is this a true reflection of how prisoners are treated, or is it a myth? Winston Churchill once stated in 1910 that we can judge a society by the way it treats its prisoners. My own experiences, and what I have witnessed first-hand of how prisoners are treated, leave a lot to be desired and go completely against the sentiments of Winston Churchill – and, more notably, Prison Service policy.

This book will give you an insight into what it is really like to be in prison on a day-to-day basis and how the system actually works. My book will also expose the racism which exists within the prison system and abuses by prison officers against inmates: namely being assaulted and threatened. Furthermore, it will show you how the incentive and privilege scheme works and the way it is abused. I will also be showing the other side of the coin in relation to prison officers: the constant threat they face from violent inmates and having to deal with the deaths of prisoners – varying from suicide to actual murder of one inmate by another. I wrote this book because I felt I could make a difference. I hope the Government will take notice of what is wrong with the system and make a change for the better.

Michael O'Brien

1

ON ARRIVAL

WHEN I ARRIVED at Cardiff Prison I did not know what to expect. I knew my emotions, and the apprehension I felt was filled with fear of the unknown – just like many other people who have never been into prison. Whether you are innocent or guilty doesn't come into it: fear of the unknown is very scary indeed for each and every one of us.

I was taken to the prison reception and was processed by the officers and given prison issue clothes to wear. I was able to have a shower beforehand and my own clothes were stored in a box with my name and number on it. I was then given a prison number; mine was W9211. I was taken to one of the prison wings, but in my case it was the prison hospital wing.

I recall how I felt when I was taken over to the hospital wing. I was feeling very suicidal and, because of this, was put into what they call a strip cell with only a mattress and a blanket. If this was supposed to stop me from feeling suicidal it had the opposite effect and made me feel worse. It felt as though I was being punished even more because I felt suicidal. But then, wouldn't anyone feel suicidal if they were charged with a murder and robbery they didn't commit?

My first impressions of the prison officers were that they were uncaring. Prison conditions were not good at Cardiff in those days. I remember having a bucket with a lid on it to use as a toilet; it was there that I'd urinate and have a crap. It was one of the most degrading things I had to do and I felt it stripped me of my dignity completely. As a Category A prisoner in the hospital wing, if I had visitors or went out of the hospital wing for any reason, I had to be accompanied by at least two prison officers. Everywhere I went was recorded in a book: what time I left and came back – it was so unreal. A few weeks after my arrival I was told by one of the officers that I was going on 'normal location' in the young offenders' wing because I was under 21. Once again I felt immediately scared of the unknown – not knowing what to expect. In a cell in the young offenders' part of the prison I was locked up for 23 hours a day, basically in a hole in a wall, and was not allowed to mix with other prisoners. Having very little contact with other people drove me crazy, and I felt it was very inhumane of the authorities to treat me like this.

For the first month of my incarceration the only people I saw were prison officers. Later I was allowed to mix with other inmates: we were allowed half-an-hour of exercise and were allowed to watch TV on alternate days. This was not really much comfort for me because, in my mind, I shouldn't have been there in the first place and I tried to make the most of it in difficult circumstances. Prison was quite grim. Cardiff was an old Victorian jail and at that time needed serious modernisation (which has now been completed) and better facilities.

The regime was quite harsh, especially if you didn't have a job. Prison regimes vary from prison to prison. At Cardiff the day began at about 7.30 a.m. when inmates went and got their breakfast. They were then locked in their cells again, but those who had jobs would have their cells opened at about 9 a.m. to start work. Two particular jobs I remember at Cardiff were the weaver's shop and peeling copper wire, which were very mundane and annoying.

Inmates would come back from their work in time for dinner and would then get banged up for approximately one hour so that the officers could have their dinner. When the officers returned from lunch the ones who had jobs to go to would be sent back to work until teatime. Some inmates would have visits from their family and the visiting rules varied for remand prisoners awaiting trial and for those who were convicted.

Remand prisoners were entitled to a fifteen-minute visit every day from their family, while those convicted had to send out what is known as a visiting order – they would get one of these each month. After coming back from work or their visits, prisoners would collect their tea and were usually put back in their cells for the night – unless it was your turn to watch a bit of TV. Sometimes you might be lucky enough to go to the gym, although this was very rare.

At about 8 p.m., two inmates with a prison officer would come round and pour a cup of tea in those awful blue plastic mugs they gave you. On a Sunday it would be coffee instead of tea. It was like drinking diesel: nasty as fuck and not one that your mother made for you, that's for sure. The authorities would probably get done for it now under the health and safety rules!

When I turned 21, I had to leave the young offenders' institute and was transferred to the main part of Cardiff Prison with the adult prisoners. In total I spent 16 months at Cardiff Prison from the time I was on remand until the time when I was convicted. During my first spell at Cardiff Prison I didn't have many problems with the prison officers. I was unhappy and disappointed to be told that I was being moved to another prison because, at that time, I was going through a messy divorce and naturally wanted to sort this out but circumstances wouldn't let me.

During my first time at Cardiff, some of the officers were really sympathetic towards me. I can recall the time when my wife bought a gold chain for our daughter, who later died through cot death, and I smuggled the chain into the prison during a visit to remind me of her. I was caught and it was confiscated from me by the officers. I expected to be placed on a prison disciplinary charge of having an unlawful article in my possession. However, when I came back from the visiting room I was called into the office where a senior prison officer, O'Brien, said to me: "Listen, I know what has happened in relation to your daughter but you shouldn't be bringing in things through visits. There are normal channels to go through. Don't let me hear of you doing this again." He then gave me the chain and tears welled up in my eyes. I thanked him profusely and left.

It would be another eight years before I went back to Cardiff Prison. This time was in relation to my stepfather's funeral – and what a change I saw in the attitudes of prison officers towards me when I arrived! By now, I had educated myself in law and prisoners' rights and my reputation had obviously preceded me. I was taken down to the segregation unit, which is a prison within a prison, because I refused Prison Officer Evans' order to bend down so he could look up my anal passage to see if I had any contraband. I refused because it was an unlawful order, and I quoted them the law under the Human Rights Act, Article 3, which states that no one shall be subjected to inhumane and degrading treatment. Not only did they not like this, but the officers' hostility towards me increased. I was subjected to threats and verbal abuse and the officers did everything they could to provoke me, such as kicking food out of my hand.

In the morning things escalated further when I was in the reception area putting my clothes on for the funeral. The officers threw the clothes on the floor, laughed and goaded me. At the church funeral service, the officers were laughing and were told to be quiet. However, the real trouble started when we arrived at the cemetery; the prison officers with me phoned the police and said there was going to be trouble at the graveside. There were armed police everywhere and it took some time before the cemetery attendant let the funeral go ahead. After reassurances from my family the authorities treated me like I was some kind of mafia man. This behaviour shouldn't have come as a surprise. By that time I had done nearly ten years in prison and in every prison I had been I had encountered harassment, bullying and abuse from the prison officers.

It was clear that the officers did not want me at Cardiff because of my high profile and the fact that they were scared that I would speak out to the media, expose their system of bullying inmates and that I would help prisoners with their rights. The whole prison system has a lot to hide and when I'd earlier taken my case to court to have access to the media, the authorities fought to keep the blanket ban on journalists visiting prisoners because they didn't want the outside world to find out about what actually goes on behind prison walls.

One of the things which causes me great concern is the issue of the strip searching of prisoners. There is no doubt that this may be necessary occasionally. However, it is used excessively at times by prison officers, just to humiliate a prisoner. Furthermore, the officers carry out an illegal procedure in relation to strip searching called squatting (looking up the anal passage, as mentioned earlier). Any prisoner who doesn't comply with squatting is subjected to violence from the prison officers and is then dragged into what is called a strip cell and left for hours without any clothes and in total humiliation.

This kind of abuse has to stop and any prisoner who is asked to squat should refuse to do it. If they are then subjected to violence from the prison officers, the prisoner can sue the Home Office for assault and inhumane and degrading treatment, torture and punishment. Squatting is illegal, full stop. The definition of Article 3 states that no one shall be subjected to inhumane or degrading treatment, torture or punishment, i.e. inhumane treatment causing very serious and cruel suffering. More specifically, the European Commission of Human Rights has defined this as follows: "Any treatment which deliberately causes severe suffering, mental or physical which in the particular situation is unjustifiable."

Degrading treatment or punishment is caused if it grossly humiliates a person before others; drives him to act against his will or his conscience; if it constitutes an insult to the prisoners' human dignity; or if it is designed to arouse in victims feelings of fear, anguish and inferiority capable of humiliating and debasing them and possibly breaking moral resistance. Yet at segregation units across the country prison officers fail to comply with this and do exactly what Article 3 tells them not to.

When I came out of prison I still encountered problems with Cardiff Prison. When I went to get a signature from a prisoner so that I could work on his case, the officer stopped me from doing so. I told him I was from the Miscarriage of Justice Organisation. He said he didn't give a fuck what organisation I was from and said: "I'm a member of the POA [Prison Officers' Association] and my organisation is bigger than yours." I turned round and said: "I know about your organisation. Some of your members beat up inmates down the segregation unit." He didn't like that, not that I gave a flying fuck: I was speaking the truth. In a nutshell, the prison officers obstructed justice and I went to *The South Wales Echo* about it. They then made false allegations against me after I'd made a complaint about it and suggested that I'd caused the trouble. They said they had investigated my complaint and, not surprisingly, it was a whitewash which covered up for the officer concerned. I had witnesses with me at the time and, as far as I know, the prison didn't even take statements from them all. I did go back to Cardiff Prison to visit a friend of mine who I believed to be innocent. His name was Nick Tucker and I visited him until he got moved but I always made sure that I was with someone like my girlfriend so they couldn't make any false allegations against me again.

I never had any trouble visiting Nick Tucker but some of the inmates I met on visits (and since they have left Cardiff Prison) have told me that inmates do get regularly beaten up in that particular segregation unit. It comes as no surprise to me and this is just one prison among many who do this throughout the country with no accountability whatsoever. It's the inmate's word against a number of prison officers and, unless the inmate has some kind of injuries, how can he or she prove that he or she has been beaten up?

Prisons are hidden from the outside world. Prison is, and still remains, a secret society where the public see and hear nothing. As I'm writing this book a TV documentary is being shown on the BBC in relation to Cardiff Prison, which gives a false view of how prison life is, mostly from the prison officer's point of view. One Cardiff inmate did give his views but he was certainly handpicked by the authorities, just as with Princess Anne's visit to Cardiff Prison when I was there. Again, the inmates were handpicked to speak to her: ones who wouldn't rock the boat or tell the truth about what actually goes on in prisons. The authorities are hardly likely to let an inmate go on television to say how he has been beaten up or harassed by the prison officers, are they?

Cardiff Prison may argue that things have changed since I was there. However, since my release, a number of inmates who have left Cardiff Prison have told me that they too were assaulted while in prison. So what has really changed in 20 years? Between 28 and 30 June 2010, the Chief Inspector of Prisons visited the prison and wrote a report which was published on 17 December 2010. In the report he exercised his concerns, stating that there was too little care in planning for vulnerable prisoners and those struggling to cope; some aspects of the management of diversity were underdeveloped and the staff struggled to deal with the churn of prisoners they faced. The Inspector of Prisons also noted the high rate of deaths in custody and also a couple of other matters regarding cleanliness of the prison and poor visitor facilities. Personally, I do not think this report went far enough. Firstly, there was no mention of the segregation unit, the bullying ground for prison officers to mistreat the prisoners, or the fact that the prison is run by members of the Prison Officers' Association in a heavy-handed manner. No mention was made either of the fact that some prison officers work with the police to give false evidence against a prisoner, which has happened on occasions, including my own case.

2

PRISON VISITS

PRISONERS ARE ALLOWED visits from their family and friends, although it varies from prison to prison as to how many visits a prisoner can have. However, in relation to the legal obligations on the prison authorities, prisoners are entitled to two visits a month. The prisoner has to make an application to one of the officers on the wing for a visiting order. The inmate has to write the names and addresses of those he wants to visit and the visiting orders get sent out. The visitors have 28 days to use the visiting order before it expires.

Visitors also have to phone the prison to book their visit, although legally all that is required for a person to visit a prisoner is a valid visiting order and some identification. The booking system was set up to give the authorities an indication of how many people would be visiting the prison each day so that they knew how many staff they would need to patrol the visiting room. However, this booking system has been abused across the country, at prisons including Cardiff, Long Lartin, and Whitmoor to name but a few. They illegally turn away visitors (some of whom have travelled miles to see their loved ones) just because they have not booked a visit. It is not a legal requirement to book a visit and the authorities have no legal right whatsoever to turn away visitors who have a valid visiting order and form of identification.

The prison officers bully the visitors into doing what they want by telling them that if they haven't booked a visit they will not see their relative. The prison service needs to address this issue, especially in the light of the case of *Raymond* v. *Honey*, which states that prisoners maintain all their civil rights in prison unless Parliament has expressly decided to take them away from the individual.

Prison authorities do not have the right to make up rules which impinge upon prisoners' rights. The turning away of visitors who have not booked a visit is illegal and it needs to be challenged by way of a judicial review because these actions are clearly unreasonable. Sometimes it can take three days to book a visit and I've had many complaints about the delays in getting through to book visits. I hope someone challenges this practice to get it abolished once and for all.

Visiting times vary from prison to prison and in some prisons you can earn an extra two visits a month. These are called privileged visits and can be taken away at any time for bad behaviour. The extra visiting rights are part of the Incentive and Privilege Scheme which I will explain later in this book.

One of the biggest problems facing prison officers in relation to visits is the serious problem of drugs and I have a great deal of sympathy for them. Some visitors will go to extreme lengths to bring drugs into the prison for their loved ones. Some of the methods used are deplorable. Take, for instance, drugs being smuggled in via a baby wearing a nappy. This was a common occurrence for some years until the authorities rumbled it. There was also a case of a woman bringing in drugs in her vagina. However, the most common way of bringing in drugs was in the visitor's mouth: a woman would kiss her husband or boyfriend and pass the drugs from her mouth to her partner's mouth. Anyone caught bringing drugs to the prisons, especially class A drugs, should face the sternest possible sentence, in order to deter others from doing so. Moreover, anyone using kids to bring in drugs should face an even harsher sentence for the very same reason.

Prisoners are obviously entitled to receive visits from their solicitors. Again, the times at which solicitors can visit varies from prison to prison. As far as I'm aware, the authorities very rarely impede a solicitor coming to visit his or her client unless they believe the solicitor is engaged in criminal activity. I never had any problems with the authorities with regard to access to my lawyer, nor do I know of any other inmate who has had this problem.

While I was at Long Lartin, however, I did encounter significant problems with the prison authorities regarding my right to have visits from journalists. Karen Voisey, from a BBC Wales current affairs programme, came up to see me after I wrote her a letter protesting my innocence. I had a few visits without any problems – that was until the authorities found out that Karen was a journalist.

They then tried to get her to sign a disclaimer to say that any material she gathered during visits would not be used for broadcast. This flew in the face of what she was trying to do: namely, investigate my case to create a television programme. She was refused entry into the prison, which hampered the story as we couldn't go through the material together. I was so infuriated that I took legal action against the then Home Secretary, Michael Howard, and the then Long Lartin prison governor, John Mullins, citing my right to free speech under Article 10 of the European Convention on Human Rights.

My case was consolidated when another prisoner had the same problems with regard to access to journalists. We both later won our case at the High Court against the Home Secretary and the prison governor. However, it wasn't without a price. For my trouble, I was shipped out to another prison on the Scottish borders, 350 miles away from family and friends. This also made it more difficult for the media to visit me. When the Labour Government came to power in 1997 it decided to appeal the decision to allow prisoners access to journalists and Jack Straw, the then Home Secretary, won at the Court of Appeal.

I then decided to appeal to the House of Lords. Before the case came before the Lords, I had already been released on bail pending my appeal for my wrongful conviction. I later won my case at the House of Lords, although it was too late for me as I was now a free man and could talk to the media without restraint anyway. However, it benefited the many innocent people who were imprisoned wrongly and who now were in a position to have journalists visit them to try and overturn their case.

The evidence which Karen Voisey and the *Week In Week Out* team found in my case, and which resulted in my case being overturned at the Appeal Courts, should be a lesson to the prison authorities not to interfere with prisoners' legal right to enlist journalists to investigate their cases. Had the prison authorities, Jack Straw and Michael Howard had their way, I would probably still be in prison now. It has, however, been brought to my attention that prison governors are still refusing to comply with the House of Lords judgment on prisoners having access to journalists.

One prisoner told me that he was only allowed one allocated journalist and that he was not allowed to contact any others. This is a clear breach of the House of Lords judgment. The governors of prisons and the Home Secretary do not have the legal power to restrict access to journalists. If they do restrict such access, they are in contempt of court and I would advise taking legal action against them to enforce the rights laid down by the courts in *O'Brien and Simms* v. *Home Secretary of State Department* (House of Lords, July 1999). Prisoners must not listen to any excuses from the governors in relation to journalists: their permission to speak to journalists is not necessary. The new standing orders in relation to journalists have no legal status whatsoever. They cannot force you to sign undertakings to ban journalists from highlighting cases. You do not need to make an application to the governor to have a visit from a journalist as described in the standing orders.

Having access to journalists is not a privilege: it's a basic human right, and the legal requirement is a valid visiting order. I reiterate that you do not have to ask for permission from the governor or anyone else in the prison authority in order to speak to a journalist. Anyone making you do so would be in contempt of court.

3

CATEGORY A PRISONS

THERE ARE FOUR categories of prisons: Category A prisons – known as dispersal prisons for high security prisoners; training prisons for long-term prisoners who do not need the highest security; Category C prisons – which are closed but have less internal security, and finally Open prisons – for prisoners who are not believed to be a risk to the public or in danger of escaping.

Male and female prisoners will be held completely separately from each other, although this may sometimes be in the same prison. Immediately after conviction, a male prisoner will be held at a local prison while his security categorisation and allocation are decided. Because there are fewer young offenders and women prisoners, the arrangements for them are not exactly the same. Women's prisons and young offenders' institutions are simply divided into open and closed establishments, although as the number of women prisoners has increased they are increasingly designating some women's prisons to be less secure and more on a par with male Category C prisons.

Categorisation

There are four security categories for adult males:

Category A: Prisoners whose escape would be highly dangerous to the public, police or security of the state and for whom the aim must be to make escape impossible.

Category B: Prisoners who do not need the highest conditions of security but for whom escape must be made very difficult.

Category C: Prisoners who cannot be trusted in open conditions but who do not have the ability or resources to make a determined escape attempt.

Category D: Prisoners who can reasonably be trusted to serve their sentences in open conditions.

Category A prisoners also have an escape risk classification based on their ability and likelihood to escape. These classifications are exceptional, high and standard escape risk. Category A prisoners have greater restrictions upon them for security reasons, and their visitors will be vetted by the police on behalf of the prison authorities. These prisoners are entitled to a formal annual review of their security categorisation during which the reports prepared on them will be disclosed and the prisoner invited to make written representations to the decision-making committee. Legal advice and assistance can be sought in making these written representations. Women prisoners and young offenders may be made

Category A, but normally they will either be allocated to open or closed conditions.

The governor makes all other categorisation decisions, be it B, C or D. Any prisoner can make a complaint to the ombudsman if the decision is considered to be unfair. Alternatively, he or she can apply to the High Court for a judicial review of his or her categorisation if there is evidence that it has been arrived at unlawfully, for example, by taking account of irrelevant information or by applying the wrong criteria.

There are five Category A prisons which hold the most dangerous prisoners in the country. These are: Long Lartin Prison in Evesham, Worcestershire; Full Sutton in Yorkshire; Whitmoor in Cambridgeshire, Frankland in Durham, and Belmarsh in London. Gartree in Leicestershire was a Category A prison but has now been downgraded to a Category B prison. I was unfortunate enough to stay at three of these establishments and I experienced bullying and fear at each, first hand.

You have to be mentally tough to survive at these establishments: the weak don't last long there at all. Within these prisons are special units known to inmates as segregation units, as already mentioned. Prisoners are segregated from other prisoners for various offences in breach of the prison discipline code. These range from assaults on other prisoners to attacks on prison officers or failing to obey a prison officer's request to do something. There are also many other offences for which a prisoner can find himself the subject of prison discipline, including false charges made by a prison officer – which do occur on a regular basis.

If a prison officer wants to place a prisoner on a 'charge', he has to describe the alleged offence on a form which is then handed to the prisoner. The prisoner then has to go before a governor to answer the charge laid against him. The prisoner can call witnesses to back up his defence and has a limited opportunity to present his case.

The governors, however, usually find the prisoner guilty regardless of the evidence and if it's a prisoner's word against a prison officer's the governors, without fail, will believe the officers. This leads to many injustices. The whole process of the governor being judge and jury is a biased one and is not independent in any way. There should be a complete independent tribunal set up to deal with prison discipline to make it fairer.

Prisoners do have access to a complaints system if they are not happy with decisions. However, the delays in relation to the complaint system take months and often the complaint is dismissed in any event. To say the complaints system is biased is an understatement. The prison authorities sweep things under the carpet on a regular basis and, again, there should be an independent tribunal to look at the complaints of prisoners. Furthermore, when an inmate puts in a complaint of an assault by an officer he is victimised. He is often bullied and threatened that it will be worse next time and immense pressure is put on the prisoner to withdraw his complaint.

Sometimes officers do speak out about what

goes on in prison. However when they do, they get victimised and ostracised by their colleagues, making it impossible to stay in their jobs. Recently, a former prison officer, Carol Lingard, who was treated as a grass after she reported bullying and intimidation of inmates, won £477,600 compensation at a Leeds tribunal. Mrs Lingard was awarded this money for victimisation and constructive dismissal after she complained about another officer at Wakefield Prison. The award was to cover for her loss of pension and income and took into account injury to her feelings.

The 67-page judgment of the Leeds tribunal lambasted the Prison Service for its handling of the case. At the time Mrs Lingard stated: "I received an unreserved apology from the Director General, Phil Wheatley, in April 2005 and I'm disappointed that despite giving the Prison Service many opportunities to take responsibility for their actions during the last three years, I have had to fight a very long and hard case at tribunal and face two tribunal hearings for this to happen."

The complaints of Mrs Lingard were based on the serious conduct of one particular officer who, she claimed, had warned a sex offender that he could be seriously hurt by other inmates if he was ever found with photos of children. Mrs Lingard alleged that this officer tried to plant evidence in his cell.

The second complaint centred on the officer who, it was alleged, changed the prisoner's records to indicate that he had a record of poor behaviour. It was further alleged that this officer was involved in a very suspicious assault allegation concerning the same prisoner. Mrs Lingard claimed that she was intimidated and discriminated against and that she was ostracised by her colleagues. She was, by then, expecting a baby and was basically forced to resign because the work environment was unsafe and hostile. She'd already served 15 years in the Prison Service.

An investigation was carried out but the tribunal described it as unprofessional and very poor. The investigation was a whitewash and found no evidence to support her claims. The governor did set up a new unit to deal with whistle-blowing cases, however, Mrs Lingard's complaints fell on deaf ears and went no further. In a statement her solicitor, John Sturzaker – who is also her brother – of law firm Russell Jones & Walker, said:

> Mrs Lingard was a respected officer who disclosed information highlighting serious wrongdoings on D Wing at HMP Wakefield. Her concerns and complaints were mishandled appallingly and she felt she had to resign her post. Mrs Lingard has now been completely vindicated by the tribunal. In their first decision the tribunal made damning criticisms of the handling of her case by the Prison Service at all levels up to and including the deputy director. In their second decision the tribunal has emphasised how good her career prospects within the service were and how much she has lost as the result of the actions of the Prison Service.

What this officer did to expose the things which were happening at HMP Wakefield was very courageous but she paid for it with her job. This is very unfair, and so is calling her a whistle-blower. This terminology stinks and makes her out to be the bad one just for telling the truth. Other officers who dare to speak out will also suffer the same fate. There are no mechanisms in place to protect prison officers who witness wrongdoing and report it. The Prison Service's attitude is, 'Shut your mouth or lose your job'. Shame on them.

I don't want the reader to think that these practices are exclusive to the top security prisons: it happens across other prisons in England and Wales and is common. I know, as I have experience of it myself as prisoner W92114 O'Brien.

The Category A prisons I've mentioned all share that common thread of bullying and intimidating prisoners who they assess as being subversive, such as someone protesting their innocence or someone who takes the authorities to court to obtain their rights. In prisons the authorities play systematic mind games, interfere with your mail from family and friends, try to provoke a reaction from you by deliberately winding you up – this is just a short list of what they try to do. This is clearly against Prison Service policy – i.e. that no officer shall provoke a prisoner – yet they do it all the time. Who is there to independently monitor whether prisoners are being abused?

There used to be what was called the Board of Visitors who were supposed to monitor prisoners' fair treatment. This has now been changed to the so-called Independent Monitoring Board. But it makes no difference what they call themselves, they do not safeguard prisoners from abuses and mostly just go along with what the authorities say. They are a toothless body who are a waste of time.

Most prisoner abuse takes place in the segregation unit. If a prisoner is placed on what is known as 'good order and discipline', he can find himself down in the segregation unit for up to 28 days. This gets reviewed every month and it is the duty of the so-called Independent Monitoring Board to review the decision of whether to renew the 28 days detention. They nearly always go along with the governor's recommendations to keep the prisoner in the segregation unit despite, in some circumstances, the prisoner not having done anything wrong. The governors have wide-ranging powers to deal with inmates in relation to breaching prison discipline, which can range from stopping them spending their prison earnings and private cash that their family has sent to them, to segregation from other prisoners for a maximum of 14 days.

The governors are legally required to give only one punishment, either loss of earnings, stoppage of canteen facilities, or segregation but the governor also has other sanctions he can use. The governors regularly dish out two or more punitive measures for the same offence. This is forbidden under the European prison rules, one of which states quite clearly that no one shall be punished for the same offence twice. However, this seems to be ignored up and down the country.

One other illegal sanction the governors impose on prisoners is stopping inmates from smoking. The prison officers confiscate the inmates' tobacco and let them go cold turkey. Anyone who smokes knows the effects this can have as cigarettes are, like drugs, very addictive. By not giving the inmates treatment to stop the cravings the authorities are torturing them by letting them go without. In turn, they are making the inmates more volatile and inflicting an assault of the mind on each and every one of them.

In a big test case which came before the courts, 200 drug-addicted prisoners sued the Government, arguing that denying them treatment (i.e. a heroin substitute), breached their human rights. The prisoners argued their rights were infringed because they were deprived of methadone and had to go what is commonly described as cold turkey. The Government had to pay compensation to them which totalled £1 million.

Six prisoners went to the High Court in 2006 claiming their rights were abused, but it was settled out of court by the Government, which paid 197 inmates in jails in England and Wales a total of £750,000. Four prisoners in Wymott jail in Lancashire received a total of £15,228 and three prisoners in Preston Prison £11,421. The compensation payments to each prisoner was about £3,807 and the cost to the taxpayer overall was £1 million, inclusive of all lawyers' fees. The Government was advised by its legal team to settle out of court to keep the costs down and save taxpayers' money. They were warned there was a real risk that if the case had gone to court, they would have had to pay the prisoners a lot more in compensation.

The prisoners had been using methadone which had been paid for by the Government but it was decided that they should go through cold turkey detoxification instead. They claimed that their human rights had been breached under Articles

3 and 14 of the European Convention on Human Rights, which bans discrimination, or inhuman or degrading treatment or punishment.

At a preliminary hearing in 2006, Richard Hermer, a human rights lawyer specialising in group actions against the Government, told the court: "Many of the prisoners were receiving methadone treatment before they entered prison and were upset at the short period of treatment using opiates they encountered in jail. Imposing the short, sharp detoxification is the issue."

The addicts said that their treatment was handled inappropriately with the consequence that they suffered injuries and had difficulties with their withdrawal. They claimed that the treatment constituted trespass and accused the Prison Service of clinical negligence. This test case is also applicable in relation to the cold turkey treatment of inmates in relation to tobacco – governors take notice!

Prison brutality is a harsh reality of prison life. When the number of prisoners who had been beaten up at Wormwood Scrubs was revealed, it didn't surprise many lawyers and former inmates. Prison brutality has been going on since at least the 1980s, if not before. Fourteen prisoners were seriously assaulted at Wormwood Scrubs in west London. The Prison Service admitted this and further admitted that officers had subjected prisoners to mock executions, death threats, sustained beatings, racist abuse and choking. This appears to be one of the biggest scandals in British legal history in relation to prisons.

HMP Wormwood Scrubs has been dogged by claims of prison brutality for many years and the Prison Service has settled out of court on another 32 cases, but did not admit any liability as to whether the claims were true. The Prison Service has paid out more than £1.7 million in compensation so far and has accepted that this could rise by a lot more. Only one case was proved until admissions in documents came about which showed that officers had brought false disciplinary charges against the prisoners to cover up the assaults.

The Prison Service accepted that top officials in management and within the prison had clearly failed to investigate the prisoners' allegations of assaults properly. Prisoners who tried to complain were beaten or threatened to keep their mouths shut. An officer who assaulted a prisoner who had been to see the chaplain said, while jumping on his ankle, "Will the chaplain help you now?"

Sir David Ramsbotham, the former Inspector of Prisons, said that if repeated warnings about brutality at the jail had been acted upon, the assaults would not have taken place. He said: "I cannot believe that the senior management of the Prison Service did not know about these assaults."

Evidence collected by lawyers in the 1990s illustrate that brutality against prisoners at HMP Wormwood Scrubs was not just a case of a few isolated incidents – it showed a big picture of widespread abuse by prison officers. The allegations led to a highly respected human rights organisation, Amnesty International, calling on the Government to order a full independent inquiry into the abuses at HMP

Wormwood Scrubs in 1998. It wanted to know what had caused the failure of the complaints system and why there wasn't anything in place to detect and deal with what it described as 'systematic abuse'. It wanted the inquiry to look at the roles of all the individuals who deal and receive the complaints, like the prison governors, the Independent Monitoring Board and everyone who may have received complaints.

As part of the inquiry, Amnesty International also wanted to look at the reasons for the failings of the Prison Service which had allowed these serious matters at HMP Wormwood Scrubs to worsen over a long period of time, despite being informed about them by different organisations. It went further and wanted the inquiry to look at ways of sorting out prison culture in relation to abuses, especially where threats of violence, bullying and intimidation prevented prisoners from making legitimate complaints.

In one of the worst incidents, an Irish inmate was pinned on a bed and choked as eight officers beat him, with one shouting that the victim should call him 'English master'. Other inmates were left with broken bones – one was so terrified that he slashed his wrists and another will need residential care to cope with the mental trauma. On several occasions officers psychologically tortured prisoners by threatening to hang them and bragged that they had done this to other inmates without being caught. Senior management knew these beatings were taking place yet they failed to do anything about it. It's the same story in other prisons, where a blind eye is turned on a regular basis.

Ethnic minorities and Irish prisoners suffer severe racism from the prison officers and it's not just confined to one prison. My experiences in Frankland Prison were quite shocking. I saw prison officers wearing National Front badges on their ties and a black friend of mine, Barrington Halstead, was beaten up at Frankland by the prison officers for daring to speak up for his rights.

One of the worst cases of racism has to be the case of Sean Higgins, who was from Birmingham and a mixed race prisoner. It was not unusual for black prisoners to suffer at the hands of prison officers, especially where the prisoner was seen as being awkward. There was also collusion from prison officials to crack down on strong-willed black prisoners.

In 2005, Mr John McGranagham, a white ex-prisoner contacted Black Britain, an anti-racist organisation, and told them all about the mistreatment being meted out to Sean Higgins. He also informed them that Sean was held in the segregation unit and repeatedly beaten up and abused. Mr McGranagham went on to say he feared for the personal safety of Mr Higgins.

Mr McGranagham strongly believed that the way in which Sean was being treated was down to sheer racism within the prison. He asked Black Britain to get involved to help Sean. Mr McGranagham contacted Sean's solicitor, Vicky King, who confirmed that Sean had been assaulted and injured by prison officers on a regular basis. Black Britain then decided to get involved.

Sean listed all the mistreatment and abuse he was subjected to by a number of racist prison officers. There was clear evidence to support Sean's allegations from photographs, medical reports and legal documents.

This was not the first time Sean had encountered such treatment. In Swaleside Prison in 1999, Sean was in his cell when a number of officers came in. They subjected him to verbal racist abuse and then used violence against him. They tried putting his neck in some sort of noose, in what can be described as a mock lynching. The police, when they came, were so shocked by Sean's injuries that they refused to take him into their custody and were adamant that he should be taken to hospital in the first instance. This was one of many attacks on him at Swaleside, which always came about after Sean put in complaints about his racist treatment at the hands of prison officers. He would not be silent on these issues, which seemed to enrage the officers even more.

Full Sutton Prison segregation unit is another known to prisoners as one where violence by the prison officers is a regular occurrence and is part of the brutal regime. Prison officers seriously hurt Sean after he dared to make complaints about the racist abuse he suffered at their hands. Sean was later charged with assaulting prison officers who needed some sort of justification for using violence against him. They basically tried to hide behind the control and restraint procedures. Sean was acquitted of all charges at Hull Crown Court. Only one conclusion can be drawn from Sean's acquittal – the prison officers lied. The jury believed Sean's defence that he was indeed mistreated and suffered at the hands of prison officers while at Full Sutton Prison. The jury also decided that Sean had a right to defend himself against sustained attacks by the prison officers.

Sean complained again of racist abuse at Frankland Prison's segregation unit – he was beaten up again by the prison officers. To cover themselves for using violence, they then made allegations that Sean had assaulted them without any provocation. Having spent time in Frankland Prison myself, I know full well that the officers don't need any excuse of provocation to assault you. They are a bunch of bullies who think they can get away with whatever they like. Sean is now taking legal action against the Prison Service and is seeking damages for what he has been through.

Sean's case is not an isolated incident. If you are of black or Asian origin you can expect to be discriminated against at some stage during your sentence. There seems to be a whole culture of racism within the system which needs to be looked at.

Solicitor Dan Rubenstein, whose firm specialises in prison litigation, has claimed that a strong culture of racism exists not just among basic grade prison officers but also within senior management of the prison department. According to Mr Rubenstein, the Prison Department is notoriously slow in responding to letters detailing claims on behalf of prisoners. He says: "They have never taken less than four months to respond." He describes follow-up action by the system into complaints of racial discrimination as being "very patchy indeed", and believes that senior management has been directly involved in racially discriminatory actions. He also claims that black prisoners who have made complaints of racial discrimination were constantly transferred. He added: "Instead of the grievance being dealt with there and then they just pass the 'problem' onto someone else."

Felix Martin, ex-prisoner and chair of the Prisoners' Race Discrimination Unit, told Black Britain that although complaints of racist abuse in prison were high, they were probably the tip of an iceberg and unreflective of the true number of incidents. "A lot of black prisoners don't bother to report it and just learn to live with it," he said. Mr Martin said that racism in prisons took many forms and varied from being given smaller portions of food in the canteen to receiving a behaviour warning for pressing a cell buzzer to request a phone call. He said: "Some officers come out with racial insults and there are ones who really bully and pick on certain inmates. When a black prisoner decides to make a complaint that's when it turns into open warfare and the victimisation comes pouring in."

The Commission for Racial Equality's 2003 report stated that: "Some prison staff discourage or prevent prisoners from making race complaints" and those who plucked up the courage to speak out against discrimination "were punished or victimised for making the complaint".

In relation to the way Irish prisoners are treated, look no further that the Birmingham Six who were wrongly convicted of the Birmingham pub bombings in 1974. While at Winston Green Prison in Birmingham they were beaten black and blue. To this day not one officer has been brought to book for what they did to them. They were not the only prisoners to have been beaten up at this prison, there have been many.

Whitmoor Prison is being taken to court by prisoners for alleged racist incidents and abuse by prison officers. A number of lawyers have come together and compiled at least 13 cases that they want to take forward. The lawyers will argue that mistreatment of prisoners is a regular occurrence at the prison.

One former prisoner, who is suing the prison, said: "In places like Whitmoor it becomes apparent that prison officers don't mix with black people. For some reason they see us as some kind of threat and regularly stereotype black people." It appears the only black people they regularly have contact with are prisoners.

This prisoner explains that while he was at Whitmoor Prison, he was put in a strip cell. Officers then started hurling racist remarks about him and his mother. He felt frightened that they could seriously harm him and realised he couldn't do anything if they did.

Two prisoners at HMP Lancashire, which is for young offenders, were assaulted by prison officers and they ended up with broken bones. Lancaster Farm fared no better and a prisoner had his arm and shoulder broken by prison officers after they hid behind control and restraint techniques. One prisoner had a dislocated wrist and another prisoner ended up with lumps and bumps on his head.

One thing which has become clear is that even young offenders do not escape from abuse of power by prison officers. I can also remember *The Independent on Sunday* getting hold of a report which was quite damaging to the Prison Service in relation to young offenders. It basically said that abuse in young offenders' prisons was rife and that the methods used were to force fists into their ribs, punch prisoners in the face, and bend back their limbs and thumbs to breaking point. It went on to say that it was believed that a couple of thousand of these kinds of assaults were happening year in, year out. Some of these prisoners end up in hospital for various treatments because of the abuse. There should have been a judicial inquiry into these matters, although, as far as I'm aware, nothing was ever done about this.

The then Chief Inspector of Prisons, Ann Owers, said she believed prison officers put their heads together and carried out serious assaults on vulnerable prisoners at High Down Prison in Sutton, Surrey. Some were actually attacked by the prison officers only a couple of days before she visited and she expressed her concern about the volume of prisoners reporting prison abuse. She went on to say that the governor took swift action against the officer concerned and she commended him/her for doing so. However, she did feel that there were still concerns about prisoners' safety which needed to be addressed.

In a survey carried out by inspectors, 32 per cent of prisoners said that they had been intimidated by staff at High Down, compared with an average of 25 per cent at other jails. There was a history of over-use of force and special cells by staff according to the report on the 740-inmate jail. Responses to the serious problem of prisoner-on-prisoner bullying had been inadequate, it added.

The use of the adjudication system which is designed to punish prisoners for prison discipline regularly gets abused. Many inmates are put on various false charges by disgruntled prison officers who dislike the inmate and who, it seems, have nothing better to do than single out prisoners. I was placed on a number of false charges at two top security prisons: Long Lartin and Gartree. On 17 February 1994 I was put on a false charge of threatening a prison officer. This officer actually attacked me with two others; they dragged me down to the segregation unit, ripped all my clothes off me and left me in a strip cell with no clothes on. The officer threatened me and all I did was stick up for myself. Luckily for me another prison officer saw what happened and when I went before the governor to answer these false charges, he had a quiet word with the governor and pointed out what the other officers had done and I was acquitted. The prison officer should have been charged by the police with assault, yet he got away scot-free. This officer also assaulted my co-accused, Ellis Sherwood, sometime later and again he got away with it.

Another charge I was placed on was for refusing to go to work. This was another illegal charge. Firstly, work is only a privilege not a right. I've never known any prisoner placed on report for a privilege – just me. And, more importantly, I had a right – as defined under Article 6 of the European Convention on Human Rights – to work on my case as much as I wished to try to prove my innocence. They denied me that right and I was placed on this charge on four separate occasions in different prisons. Each time I proved my case and I was acquitted by the prison service.

I was then accused on one occasion of being abusive to Prison Officer Helen Gilbert. This officer had it in for me for some reason. She didn't tell the governor that she came into my cell and deliberately woke me up by poking me in the chest and, yes, I did have a go at her. I said to her that I would sue her for assault. Nothing else was said. I was found guilty by Governor Barton and, as punishment, was deducted £3 out of my wages. I was so incensed that I appealed this decision and eventually got this dodgy verdict overturned.

The silliest charge I've ever been placed on was when I handed a County Court summons to Officer Helen Gilbert for assaulting me. They placed me on another illegal charge of delivering to any person an unauthorised article. This was a legal article and I was well within my rights to instigate legal proceedings against her. I accept that I went about it in the wrong way, but it is difficult to do things right when you are constantly being harassed from those who are supposed to protect you.

Another example of the adjudication process being abused and illegally used against me was when I had a visit from my family. I took my legal papers to the visiting room, as I normally do, when I was approached by a prison officer. He took my legal papers away from me and refused to give them back.

I went up to him and took them back off him and I was charged with taking my legal papers back off the officer without permission. The documents had legal privilege and he was in the wrong for taking them. It came as no surprise that I was found not guilty, yet again.

My co-accused, Ellis Sherwood, was in Whitmoor Prison and told me of many things that went on in the segregation unit. When a prison officer approached a prisoner cell, you would be told to stand against the wall where they could see you. If the prisoner didn't comply, the officers would rush into the cell and drag the inmate to the floor, out of the cell, and put them into the strip cell and then take all the clothes from the prisoner, leaving him naked. How can this behaviour be legal or even justified? It's abuse at the highest level.

An outside body should be set up which can access prisons day and night, without warning, to inspect the prison and the prisoners. Only then, maybe, will we uncover some of the mistreatment of prisoners. Without this independent body abuses against prisoners are going to continue and be hushed up behind closed doors – a truly secret society.

Prisoner Charles Hanson gives his take on the prison system:

> Political correctness: given the nature of the joyless, elitist and purist politically correct ideology has crept into every facet of our lives and in its wake, crushes dissent, and glorifies victimhood. With its authoritarian and rigid thought-police control over our lives, not least in the Prison Service, this dogma, indeed creed, ostensibly designed to protect disadvantaged groups, is actually all

about advertising the moral purity of those who enforce it. It also comes nicely wrapped up in a language all of its own so that the various definitions of the mumbo-jumbo language often leaves many people bewildered as to render the language meaningless. One man's sense, of course, is another man's nonsense.

I have a different take on the A to Z of the politically correct ethos which underlines Prison Service policy and it goes something like this:

A: After-care A noble and worthy idea but an idea it remains as after-care often means something entirely different. For example, probation hostels are often dumps and, at worst, an extension of the prison one has left behind. After-care can also mean recall to prison as the Probation Service systematically fails offenders and creates more hardened and incorrigible offenders.

B: Board of Visitors Now known as the Independent Monitoring Board, a useless body of local do-gooders, whose egos are bigger than anything they ever achieve for prisoners and who are likely to be found hobnobbing with the governor over tea and biscuits or at the local golf course with the same.

C: Categorisation A system where prisoners are pigeon-holed according to their offence and past history. Not exactly scientific but can work wonders for the grass or tea boy who can move rapidly through the system and be rewarded with a lower category status, thus attracting an easy passage through his sentence. For most prisoners, it becomes a hit-and-miss affair.

D: Diversity The Prison Service obsession, where prisoners are again pigeon-holed according to their ethnic origins or religious background. No other groups are worthy of consideration, so that diversity actually means division and divisiveness, the opposite of equality and cohesion – where some prisoners are more equal than others. In the Prison Service, diversity means what staff want it to mean, with every group trying to grab a bit of the action.

E: Education A standing joke as education departments in their politically correct target-driven culture sacrifices prisoners' actual needs and disregards what would actually benefit prisoners – a venue for social engineering and thought control. For long-serving prisoners, Ofsted (Office for Standards in Education) reported in January 2009 that they were being failed and their needs were not being met. Education managers remain unmoved as they continue to draw generous salaries for often meaningless programmes.

F: Funding Everything within the Prison Service is determined by funding and budgets. Prison governors can, and do, limit opportunities for prisoners to save a few quid and cut back on facilities so that the revolving door of offending is maintained. Job security, however, is unaffected.

G: GOAD (Good Order and Discipline) A device for prison governors to remove from the prison population those prisoners who are deemed to be a threat to the *status quo* – translated as being prisoners who are radical and up for a challenge to injustice, unfairness or prison staff brutality and bullying.

H: Health and Safety or Elf and Safety. A current phenomenon which has spawned a gigantic industry that has mushroomed out of control and provided a gravy train for its followers. All prisons have a health and safety officer and a health and safety policy. However, while health and safety is a current fad, heavily promoted and forced down our throats, two or three prisoners continue to eat, sleep and shit in the same cell designed for one. Nowhere is health and safety a consideration there.

I: Incentives and Earnings Privilege Scheme (IEPS). A system whereby prisoners are graded according to their behaviour and progress and become eligible for different grades, privileges and facilities. Often arbitrary and little more than a system of control, the IEPS scheme is designed more for the easiness of prison staff who simply want a quiet life.

J: Justice An alien concept for prison staff and one which they have little understanding of. Indeed, very few are able to spell it. Justice means many things to many people, but for prisoners it's synonymous with fair play, opportunity, freedom from pettiness and arbitrary and irrational decision-making. Prison staff also have difficulty in understanding what those terms mean.

K: KPIs (Key Performance Indicators) Another politically correct term to describe how well the prison is doing by use of graphs, pie charts, tables and columns of figures. A dubious and easily-manipulated system to bolster the governor and staff's reputation and credentials, but meaningless in the eyes of prisoners who don't need maths to figure out how chaotic the prison system really is.

L: Letters Often the only lifeline a prisoner will have to the outside world and one which is often abused by prison staff, from opening legal correspondence contrary to the rules, stealing cash from envelopes, censoring comments and thoughts of prisoners and interpreting what they mean, to noting dissent and anything perceived to be racist, sexist, and all other 'ists' and 'isms' which the politically correct are obsessed with weeding out.

M: Mandatory Drug Testing (MDT) Something all prisoners are subject to but quite often it is only those who have no drug history who will be targeted. Figures count here and, by a sleight of hand, it makes sense not to test the guilty as that would demonstrate that prison security is failing to stem the flow of drugs into prisons which, in any event, often find their way to prisoners through corrupt staff.

N: Nurses Not directly employed by HM Prison Service but by local NHS Trusts. Approach with caution, as contact can often damage your health and should rightly carry a Government health warning. Some rumoured to have worked previously in death camps, but this has not yet been confirmed!

O: Offending behaviour programmes A spoon-fed ideology which holds that prisoners can be coerced, threatened or abused into attending dubious and meaningless courses to reduce risk through changing their thinking patterns. Does an Englishman going to live in China and having to learn Chinese forget he ever spoke English?

A big money spinner for those who develop such courses and those who tutor them without there being any convincing evidence that they actually achieve what is claimed. Some 65 per cent of adult prisoners and 75 per cent of young offenders who are released from prison will reconvict within two years of their release and most of those would have undertaken such courses. Those who subscribe to the validity of and embrace such programmes disregard the inconvenient truth – they are simply no more than a 'one size cap fits all' indoctrination.

P: Prisoner's Consultative Committee A so-called democratic but politically correct committee of prison governors set up to elicit intelligence and prisoners' grievances from a select few prisoners who are usually self-assumed, self-elected and self-serving spokesmen for all other prisoners. The committee acts as a barometer of how prisoners are thinking and, in line with politically correct and KGB-like snooping, encourages a small band of prisoners to tell tales on others under the guise of seeking considerations and extra privileges for all. Governors and prison staff listen and note grievances but that is the limit of their involvement. Who cares anyway?

Q: Questionnaire Something, at one time or another, that prisoners will be required to complete. These useless pieces of paper serve no function at all except to test what prisoners think about food, healthcare or some other facility. Such pieces of paper change nothing and if they did it's a sure-fire bet that this means of testing prisoner responses would be scrapped.

R: Resettlement Something which should be the function of all prisons and not just a designated few. Resettlement, however, does not exist and is merely a description to supposedly prepare a prisoner for release. The reality is that a burglar coming into prison, unable to read and write and coerced into education, will often be released with a lesser stake in the community but will still be a burglar who is now literate.

S: Safer Custody Describes how the Prison Service has measures to reduce suicide, self-harm and bullying, but which fails miserably as record numbers of prisoners die by their own hand; mentally disordered prisoners cause harm to themselves and predatory and bullying prisoners seek to control the lives of other prisoners and do the job of prison staff.

T: Therapeutic Communities The likes of Grendon and Dovegate Prisons which supposedly challenge a prisoner's offending behaviour. They are liberal regimes and a source for researchers but do not succeed in what they claim to do. Seen by many prisoners as enhancing their prospect of parole, but sadly it is not the case. An avenue for the do-gooder elements who want to peer inside the minds of those who volunteer for such prisons.

U: Use of force A means whereby prison staff can, on the orders of prison governors, use violence against a prisoner to restrain and control him very much in line with those who had no qualms about brutalising others in Nazi Germany. Read: "I am only doing my job and am only following orders." The SS made the same claims in war crimes trials.

V: Victims Those who have been on the receiving end of offending behaviour which the politically correct do nothing about. Instead they send the perpetrators to prison so that one day they can be released to continue with their lifestyle. Fewer victims equals fewer prisoners equals fewer prison staff and fewer probation officers etc. The mathematics is simple. The industry of prisons, the Probation Service and control of others would be changed forever by any conceivable reforms to change prisons and prisoners and thus reduce the likelihood of more victims.

W: Welfare Supposedly linked to rehabilitation and so-called through-care. The politically correct world however demands that you must follow their rules on how to live, love, work, play and think with any dissent, thinking for oneself and freedom of thought and speech being treated as a cardinal sin to be challenged. The "we know what is best for others" approach has to prevail or one faces the wrath of the liberal elitist and politically correct staff who tend to dominate prison regimes and policy, and it results in attempts to socially engineer prisoners.

X: Xerox So that everyone can be bombarded with politically correct unwanted junk leaflets, questionnaires, notices for prison display boards and new rules, Xerox photocopying machines are often put into overdrive with a significant part of the prison budget being deployed to creating masses of waste paper which is then recycled for more notices, questionnaires, leaflets and rules.

Y: Young offenders The UK has the dubious distinction of locking up more young people than any other country in Europe and, along the way, the system will demonise and criminalise them at the earliest possible age and exclude them from membership of the community. The so-called liberals and politically correct in Government have no qualms about sending kids to prison to learn the ropes of offending behaviour, although they will always claim that such kids are casualties of their environment and upbringing and it's not really their fault. Who has created such environments where these kids stand no chance?

Z: Zoonosis or Zoonotic infections. Yes, last but not least the Prison Service has got everything covered and in Prison Service Order (PSO) 3805 there are instructions and advice on how to deal with those who have caught an infection from animals and that's before we get to some prison staff. Another faddish kneejerk health and safety response but familiar to the politically correct who seem to want to scare everyone to death, which is more likely the outcome than being bitten by a horse on the exercise yard.

*   *   *

It's not just adult prisoners who get mistreated. Professor Sir Al Aynsley Green, the Children's Commissioner for England, has highlighted the "overuse of restraint and force" in young offender institutions and secure training centres, and is calling for an immediate ban on the practice of painful restraint, which includes hitting children in the face, twisting their thumbs and limbs and pinning them down in painful stress positions as a form of punishment or to ensure compliance. The Government commissioned an inquiry into these controversial issues and Sir Aynsley Green said that it was totally unacceptable for vulnerable children in society to have violence used against them to punish and control them. Control and restraint methods are only supposed to be used as a very last resort. However, in 2005/6 it was used in secure training centres 3,036 times. Some of these cases were deemed so serious that they were referred to the Youth Justice Board.

Despite these secure training centres having some of the most vulnerable children, staff are trained to use physical violence to keep them subdued. The staff at these centres make out that these techniques are only used as a very last resort. However, the statistics show that this is not the case. If these techniques were used by the police or anyone else, they would be facing assault charges.

A training manual called *Physical Control in Care* exists. It details all the techniques, holds and moves to be used against children. Some of them involve a number of adults jumping on top of a child and putting them in a position that could endanger their lives. The Government have kept a lid on these techniques and have consistently refused to reveal them even though there have been many requests from journalists and lawyers to disclose them.

In secure training centres, youth offenders' institutions and secure children's homes, 2,000 cases were reported where control and restraint methods were actually used. A number of these required some form of medical treatment for different kinds of injuries.

Natalie Cronin, head of policy and public affairs at the NSPCC says: "For too long, children as young as twelve have been subjected to dangerous, violent and degrading restraint techniques in young offenders' institutions. It should not be legal for anyone to deliberately inflict pain on a child as a method of restraint."

An inquiry commissioned by the Government was set up to look at the risks of injury and death in connection with control and restraint techniques. The Children's Commissioner made some submissions and said he wanted to see a review of the whole juvenile justice system. He went on to say that he felt the restraint of children should only be used as a very last resort and only if the child posed a risk of harm to themselves and or to others. He called on staff working in this field to have extra training to safeguard the well-being of children. It is also very important to note that the methods used in these units against children are clear violations of the United Nations Convention on the Rights of the Child and clearly breach the European Convention on Human Rights.

Serious controversy arose from the sad deaths of two children while in custody. Fifteen-year-old Gareth Myatt and Adam Rickwood both died in 2004 in separate incidents at Rainbrook and Hasssockfield Secure Training Centres after being restrained by staff. In the past 17 years, 30 children have died in custody. It is thought that Adam was the youngest prisoner to die in custody. He hanged himself not long after he was subjected to control and restraint methods by staff using the controversial nose technique. Staff used what is called the 'double-seated embrace technique' on Gareth and he died of asphyxia at the hands of three staff while being restrained.

After hearing about these tragic deaths, children's charities called for these restraint methods to be withdrawn. However, the Government responded to the criticism by actually broadening the rules on control and restraint techniques, giving those in authority more power to control children in this way to ensure that good order and discipline is kept, rather than only using the minimum amount of force to prevent self-harm, escape, and being a danger to others.

The chief executive of the Youth Justice Board, Ellie Roy, gave evidence to a Parliamentary inquiry and was asked to give an account of an incident where good order and discipline were enforced. She told the inquiry that four boys who refused to go to bed and had linked arms were subjected to control and restraint methods and tried to justify it by saying things would have escalated it they had not done so.

The United Nations was told about what was going on by the Children's Rights Alliance, a body which supports a number of campaign and welfare groups in relation to children. Both hit out at the Government and said it was guilty of wilful neglect. The Government was also criticised for not implementing one of the treaties under the UN Convention on the Rights of the Child. Around the same time, the European Committee for the Prevention of Torture also took up these issues concerning children with the Labour Government of the time.

Some of the restraints could be viewed as assaults. "We're doing things to children which they don't even do in Guantanamo Bay," says Frances Crook, director of the Howard League for Penal Reform. "Painful distraction is assault and I cannot see why the police aren't involved in investigating it," she added.

The Parliamentary Joint Committee on Human Rights heard evidence from the Youth Justice Board that children in their care faced different kinds of punishments. They went on to say that they didn't have a particular method of restraint used on children at their various facilities.

The Government did decide to suspend the two most controversial restraint methods used on children. These were the 'double basket hold' and the 'nose distraction technique' and these suspensions came about after a panel of medical experts exercised their concern. There are still other methods in use to restrain children in custody, including the thumb and rib distractions, and other holds.

Dr Theodore Mutale, a consultant psychiatrist who used to be on the Youth Justice Board, believes that there is no need to use these methods on children, especially for a child previously abused. He claimed that not all cases of control and restraint on children were actually logged. The Youth Justice Board says that it wants to see less use of these restraints and is looking at other ways to deal with children. It remains to be seen if this will ever actually happen.

Pamela Wilton, the mother of Gareth Myatt, said that her life would never be the same again and was shocked by the circumstances of his death. The fact that the Youth Justice Board is looking at other methods to restrain children will be of no comfort to Pamela Wilton or Adam Rickwood's family as it won't bring their boys back.

In 2011 the jury at the second inquest into the death of 14-year-old Adam Rickwood at Hassockfield in County Durham returned a damning narrative verdict criticising the failings of Serco, the private company running Hassockfield, the Youth Justice Board, the Prison Service restraint trainers and the Lancashire youth offending team.

Following the verdict, Adam Rickwood's mother,

Carol Pounder, said: "Nothing can bring Adam back. I have waited over six years for truth and justice. All I have ever wanted is to find out the truth about what happened to my son and for those responsible for unlawful assaults to be held to account."

Acting for Carol Pounder, Mark Scott of Bhatt Murphy solicitors, said: "It has taken a six-year legal battle, including a flawed first inquest and three judicial reviews (one of which went to the Court of Appeal), to finally expose the numerous failings and illegal treatment that Adam and many other vulnerable children in privatised child prisons, have suffered."

Deborah Coles, co-director of Inquest, said:

> This is a vindication of the battle by Adam's family for the truth against a background of denial and secrecy by the Youth Justice Board and Serco. That thousands of vulnerable children were systematically subjected to unlawful restraint in privatised child prisons – and that none of the regulatory or inspection bodies of the state did anything about it – is shameful. The public scrutiny finally afforded by this properly conducted inquest into Adam's tragic death, has highlighted serious failings in the way the state treats children in conflict with the law. The state must now respond and implement meaningful changes in order to safeguard lives in future.

Maybe, just maybe, some lessons will be learnt: only time will tell.

The children's charity, Barnardo's, produced a very damning report into child custody. It found that a number of children sent to prison were in fact wrongly convicted. It also found that the number of youngsters jailed between the ages of 12 and

14 for minor offences went against Government guidelines.

Barnardo's looked at 214 cases of child incarceration and found that a significant proportion of those in this age group were sent to prison between 2007 and 2008. They stated that many of them were not repeat offenders or convicted of serious offences. The statistics for those who were sent to prison for breaching a community order was one in five.

The Barnardo's report suggests that, in England and Wales, 170 children should not have been imprisoned. It also shows that many of the children had been abused at one stage and had seen violence in the home.

Martin Narey, chief executive of Barnardo's, accepted that some children needed to be locked up, but basically believed Government and Parliament only intended to put children as young as this in prison as a very last resort.

In 1998 it would have been unlawful to place children in custody at this age yet it now happens on a regular basis, a point which Martin Narey makes in his report. I am of the view that unless a child has committed serious offences like rape or murder, there must be another way of dealing with children who break the law. Prison can destroy the minds of adult prisoners: can you imagine what it does to children?

Barnardo's want Parliament to put in place tough new rules so that children under a certain age cannot be sent to prison unless they have committed very serious offences or they continue to re-offend. They go on to say that just because a child may break a community order, they should never be sent to prison unless, of course, a violent offence is committed.

Former Liberal Democrat MP David Howarth accused the last Labour Government of being obsessed with locking up children, trying to act tough. Many children's charities agree with his sentiments and it becomes clear that something has to be done about it.

Many people believe that locking up children can lead them to pursue a life of crime once they are released, and I agree. The Government should be looking at ways to prevent children from committing crimes, rather than jailing them and making matters worse.

I believe that youth justice in Wales should be devolved to the Welsh Assembly and the Howard League for Penal Reform has made that recommendation in a report which was published recently. Elfyn Llwyd MP, who has championed many Welsh issues, welcomed this report.

The Howard League report was damning. It showed that, as of January 2009, five girls and 139 boys were in Welsh and English prisons, a total of 144 children in custody, with most, 122, in English establishments far away from their families. The Howard League stated it would support Wales having control over its own affairs on this issue, as long as it did things differently to the English system.

Elfyn Llwyd's response was:

I'm pleased that the call for youth justice to be devolved is now echoed by the well-respected Howard League. These figures are disturbingly high, as is the fact that many of these children were imprisoned far away from their homes and communities.

This report echoes what Plaid has advocated for some time. Devolving the youth justice system would allow Wales to draw on best practice from across the world and set us apart.

The devolved youth justice system is already working much better in Scotland, for example. There is no reason why Wales should not take the lead too in being able to reform its own.

Clearly the best way is to help young people early on and stop them becoming criminalised by the system. Earlier this year we discovered that over 160,000 children in the UK now have a parent in jail. The harsh reality too is that in a vicious circle, a shocking percentage of these children go on to offend themselves.

Research has also demonstrated the importance of keeping family in close proximity to have the best possible hopes of rehabilitation.

This is exactly why Plaid MPs have campaigned for so long to get a prison in north Wales. There is still no guarantee we will get one.

Prison is not an easy subject to discuss, but it is one that must be brought to the fore as the current system is clearly failing. We must look for different solutions and politicians should lead an honest and open debate on the future of our own justice system.

He went on to say that it wasn't the first time that concerns like this had been raised and that his party had always argued that Wales should have its own powers over the criminal justice system.

I endorse what Elfyn Lloyd has stated. Wales should be leading the way on prison issues and the

Welsh Assembly should have the powers to look after its own affairs on this issue. If the Assembly does get the powers required, we can stop children from being sent to prison in the first place. There must be an alternative. I'm of the view that prison is no place for children in a so-called civilised society.

*   *   *

There is very little help for children whose parents are in prison. I know that from my own experiences. There was no one to help my son Kyle from outside the family and I'm now aware of the damage a parent in prison can do to a child. It causes long-term damage which sometimes cannot be repaired. It can also lead to a child going off the rails. In my son's case, he was lucky to have caring family members to support him – not all children are in that position.

As mentioned, according to Barnardo's 160,000 children could be in that category, which is very worrying indeed. All local authorities have a duty of care to plan for such youngsters in their area. The Government, though, has let them off the hook when it comes to prisoners' children and doesn't do anything for them unless they are a special case.

Prisoners' children get treated as if they don't exist, which is very startling when you consider that they are very vulnerable and often live in extreme poverty and are unlikely to leave school with any qualifications. Antisocial behaviour is apparent in some of the children of prisoners and more must be done to help them.

The European Commissioner for Human Rights, Thomas Hammarberg, expressed his concern about locking up children in prison and went on to say that European nations lock up more children at a very young age than any other continent. He said some countries were trying to get the age limit increased and in the ex-Soviet state of Georgia they had already passed a law to do so. He felt this wasn't the way forward and made a point of seeking other solutions to the problem.

Many organisations, including the United Nations, have called for separate systems of justice for children. This does seem to be progress and if a separate system were set up it would tackle the root causes of why children commit crimes, rather than just sending them to prison and criminalising them. If you can get to the root causes of why a particular child has done something wrong and has broken the law, you will be in with a far better chance of nipping things in the bud and guiding the child away from crime. Jailing children achieves nothing and it is the system's cowardly way out instead of dealing with the real issues.

* * *

The Inspector of Prisons until 2010, Dame Anne Owers, produced a recent report and confirmed to *The Guardian* newspaper that prison officers were using more violence to control prisoners than ever before. It has been eleven years since I left prison. It's clear things haven't got any better since I was there.

In fact, it confirms what most people who work with prisoners already know: that it has got worse and, more importantly, without any accountability for those responsible.

At Parkhurst Prison in June 2001, prisoner Paul Smith was assaulted by staff. He recently won damages against the prison after the County Court disbelieved the evidence of the prison officers. Mr Smith was assaulted by a number of officers while in the segregation unit of the prison and ended up with a catalogue of injuries to his body. The judge presiding over the case in the civil courts heard the evidence over a seven-day period and concluded that the officers had been untruthful to the court as the injuries Mr Smith had received were inflicted by prison officers. Mr Smith could not prove to the court, however, that the prison officers had started the fire in his cell at dinner time, or that the behaviour of the officers in the night was a further assault. An inquiry was ordered by the Prison Service – however it was later put on hold while Hampshire police started investigating the case. Answers to police questions were not forthcoming and the case was dropped.

Why did Hampshire police not arrest the prison officers? There was enough evidence to arrest them and interview them. Prisoners have no protection from the police when assaulted by prison officers, it seems. It therefore gives prison officers a licence to do whatever they want without any redress from the law. Mr Smith had no alternative but to launch civil proceedings to get some kind of justice. He has now been vindicated. Some interesting points were raised by the judge. She reflected that there were too many inconsistencies between the prison officers' versions of events and those of the witnesses and threw out the witness statements which the Treasury solicitor tried to use.

There was identical wording over a number of paragraphs of the statements, and evidence which was contradicted by important witnesses. More damaging has to be the fact that one witness, a Mr Forman, had produced a statement using the cut and paste technique from his computer. The judge felt she could not rely on statements such as this as not all the witnesses had amended the typewritten ones. The evidence of four prison officers: a Mr Wilcox, Mr Walls, Mr Ross and Mr Entwhisle was dismissed as being unreliable as were the prison records.

According to the judge a culture of producing inaccurate reports in cases like Mr Smith's was prevalent. Following the court's verdict, Mr Smith thanked everyone and commented on the difficult task facing him in taking legal action, but he was determined to bring these officers to court and prove what they had done to him. He hoped it would deter other prison officers from behaving in this manner.

Kate Maynard, solicitor for Mr Smith, said:

> Prison officers who assault troublesome prisoners often get away with it because there is a culture of impunity in prisons. In this case, a member of the Board of Visitors, to whom Mr Smith complained immediately after the assault, instantly dismissed his complaint and failed to take any action. Records show that medical staff and the Governor were present at the time when the main assault took place, yet they took no action and still have not been brought to account. The police shelved their investigation

after the prison officers said that they would not answer
questions in interview, and an internal inquiry was
started but never concluded.

As is clear from the judgment, two key factors enabled
Mr Smith to prove his case. First, he was moved to
another prison shortly after the assault where, partly to
cover their backs, the receiving prison recorded all his
injuries on arrival, and took him to an outside hospital.
The burden then shifted on the state to account for those
injuries.

Second, the key officers that were involved in the
assault on Mr Smith were unable to sustain their
concocted story when forced to account to a court for
what happened.

Despite declaring at an earlier hearing that they 'won't
pay a penny' to Mr Smith, the Ministry of Justice
has been ordered to pay substantial damages to him,
plus interest at an enhanced rate and also his legal
costs. The damages include: aggravated damages for
the arbitrary punishment inflicted on him without
redress, which impacted adversely on his perception
of prison officers for the rest of his prison sentence
and punitive (exemplary) damages for the culture of
bad record-keeping at the prison and the failure to
reinstate the internal inquiry. Officers were not asked
to account for themselves until 2008 when they had
to produce witness statements for trial. This prevented
any remedial action from taking place to prevent a re-
occurrence, and prevented officers being brought to
task.

It is not easy trying to take prison officers to court
for wrongdoing and many obstacles are placed in
your way to stop you from doing so. These include

intimidation and routine threats of violence. However, I would encourage any prisoner who has been assaulted not to be deterred by this, and to be strong and fight for the truth to obtain justice. The more cases which come before the courts, the greater the likelihood that something will be done about these abuses. It's the only way forward.

There are times when I do, however, have sympathy with the Prison Service and for prison officers, especially in their fight against drugs and mobile phones in prison. In an extraordinary case, a prisoner started legal proceedings after bringing a mobile phone into the prison and having it confiscated by the prison officers – the phone was later destroyed at a training exercise. The prisoner is now entitled to compensation after winning his case in court. The Prison Service was quite shocked by the decision and is now appealing. The judge ruled that the phone was still the property of the prisoner and it should have been returned upon his release.

Mobile phones play a significant role in getting drugs into prison and can be used by prisoners to taunt their victims and even harass them. I always fought for prisoners' rights when I was in prison and, while I agree that the Prison Service was right to confiscate the phone, it had no right whatsoever to destroy a prisoner's property as the law is clear on this particular issue. The judge argued that this was a civil rights issue because it was still the prisoner's property and I wholeheartedly agree with the judge.

However, this judge also has no idea the problems mobile phones cause in prison. They are used to set up drug deals which have a dramatic impact on the prison. Many prisoners are hooked on cocaine and heroin. I don't know why this prisoner is even complaining about the phone being confiscated. Every prisoner knows that if you get caught with an unauthorised article, it will be confiscated. If prisoners take the risk of bringing illegal articles into the prison they know the consequences. What no one mentioned in this case was that it was a serious breach of security.

4

INCENTIVE SCHEME

THE PRISON SERVICE OPERATES a scheme of incentives and earned privileges. This means that prisoners have the opportunity to get extra privileges through good behaviour, but lose those privileges if they misbehave. While in theory this is a good idea, it is nevertheless open to abuse and is abused.

All prisoners, including non-convicted and civil prisoners, are required to be classified according to one of three categorised regimes: basic, standard or enhanced. The prison governor takes this decision based on a prisoner's performance in custody – for example, the disciplinary record. Each regime offers a different level of incentives and privileges and commonly prisoners on the basic regime will receive the legal minimum in terms of visits or access to private cash and wages. Those on the standard and enhanced regimes will receive progressively more favourable facilities, although the precise nature of these will vary according to each prison's security category. These regulations also require a number of key items such as phone cards, cigarettes and stamps to be purchased from the private cash allowance.

The privileges that can be earned affect a prisoner's daily life in prison. They include: the number of hours allowed out of their cell, the number of visits allowed above the minimum requirement, access to more of their own money to spend (on top of their prison wage) in the prison shop or on phone calls, the opportunity to wear their own clothes and to cook their own food and lastly the chance to have a television in their cell, paid for by the prisoner.

If a prisoner is placed on the basic regime it means that he is locked up for approximately 23 hours of the day, he has fewer visiting rights, and is normally deprived of newspapers and radios. On the standard regime you get more time out of the cells, have regular access to the library, possibly a job also, and have more visiting rights.

On the enhanced regime you get much more time out of your cell, access to the better jobs in the prison and further visiting rights. I have no doubt that the prison service brought in this regime with the best intentions, as we must remind ourselves that there are some prisoners who will do whatever it takes to cause trouble in prison, including assaulting prison officers. However, during my time inside, I uncovered a number of abuses of this regime which caused me great concern.

It's not difficult to find yourself on the basic regime. The prison runs a 'three strikes and you're on basic regime' system. Misdemeanours such as getting up late for work are classed as one strike. If you have a dispute with a prison officer, even if the prison officer is in the wrong, it counts as another strike, and if you don't listen to what an officer has told you, that too counts as a strike also.

Once you've accumulated three strikes the prison officers take you from standard location and, if necessary, use violence to force you to move to the basic regime if you put up a struggle. Once on the basic regime you can be there for months. Unlike in the case of a prison disciplinary offence, you don't get a hearing in order to put a defence forward. They strip you of that right on the basic regime which, in my view, is illegal.

Article 6 of the European Convention of Human Rights clearly states that anyone accused has a right to a fair hearing. Prisoners are being denied that right on the basic regime which, in my view, needs to be challenged in the courts. The basic regime has been described by many prisoners as a segregation unit with another name, and I agree.

Denying prisoners access to a radio and newspapers is also illegal. The European Court of Human Rights has already declared this to be a sensory deprivation in cases which have come before it. Sensory deprivation happens a great deal in the segregation unit. It's commonplace throughout the prison system.

Many prisoners end up on the basic regime due to failing the mandatory drug tests. Once they have failed one drug test, the inmates are subjected to more frequent tests. In some circumstances, this is justified, for example, if Class A drugs are found and if there is a link to the crime the inmate committed in the first place. But there are a number of flaws within the mandatory drugs testing system, which are a cause for concern. If an inmate has been found guilty of having drugs in his system the authorities normally retest the inmate within a 30-day period. However, I obtained a report from a renowned French doctor who specialises in drug abuse, which stated that, for a chronic smoker of cannabis, the drug stays within the body system for 77 days. If the authorities retest the inmate after only 30 days, it means that he still has the drug in his system and is actually being punished for the same offence twice. This is forbidden under European prison law.

How many inmates have fallen foul of this is open to question. However it's interesting to note that outside prison anyone who smokes cannabis can do so without any penalty from the law because the police cannot take samples from members of the public who smoke cannabis at their home; to do so would be against the person's human rights. So it could also be argued that prisoners' rights are being infringed by these drug tests. I believe that inmates who smoke cannabis shouldn't be penalised by the prison authorities because they do not go out and commit crimes to pay for their habit, unlike those on heroin and crack cocaine.

Most of the inmates who fall foul of drug testing and are placed on the basic regime are cannabis smokers. Yet heroin and cocaine addicts seem to escape any punishment due to the fact these drugs remain in the body for only about three to four days. Prisoners addicted to heroin and crack cocaine are more likely to re-offend once released. These are the prisoners who should be targeted by the authorities.

I feel there should be a independent body set up to monitor the prison incentive scheme which has the power to return prisoners to 'normal location' and which, if abuses of the scheme become apparent, is able to rectify those matters speedily and fairly.

Most of the drugs which come in to prison do not come through prisoners' visitors, despite what the authorities would like you to believe. Although some visitors do bring in drugs, a lot comes through other means – namely prison officers. Former prison officer, Gordon Hacker, has admitted conspiring to smuggle cannabis into HMP Rye Hill between November 2004 and April 2005. He passed on information to the prisoners about the times drugs were to be thrown over the prison wall. Hacker was jailed, as was Prison Officer Mark Berry, for supplying drugs to a prisoner.

I recall a prison officer who used to work in the library at Long Lartin Prison. He used to change money for prisoners. Prisoners would get their wages paid in cash in those days, mostly 50p pieces. Prisoners used to smuggle in paper money and then take it to this officer to change the money into 50p pieces. You got £7 worth of coins for every tenner you gave him, making him a profit of £3. It took years before he was actually caught and it was rumoured that he made so much money that he paid his mortgage off. Due to a blunder by prison officials at the prison, he even walked away from his job without any charges being brought.

The Metropolitan Police have recognised there is a serious problem with prison officers bringing contraband into prisons, and there was talk a long time ago about organising a special unit to tackle this problem. But, as far as I'm aware this unit has never got off the ground.

From the amount of drugs I saw in prison it was improbable that such a large quantity of drugs had been brought in through prison visitors, especially as visiting rooms in nearly all prisons have CCTV cameras.

It was once estimated that one in ten prison officers were corrupt. A new unit was supposed to tackle corrupt officers and stop them from bringing drugs and mobile phones into prisons. A former high-ranking prison official once estimated that more than £100 million worth of drugs was changing hands in prisons every year, and that the majority of the drugs, as well as other items, were brought into prison by officers. A couple of years ago, a woman prison officer alleged that at least 30 prison officers at Pentonville Prison were corrupt. The allegations included smuggling a gun into a prisoner's cell, officers taking and supplying drugs to the prisoners, and also assistance with planning escapes. Fourteen officers were suspended pending further inquiries.

Usually I don't have any time for the Independent Monitoring Board, however, on one occasion it did highlight the supply of mobile phones being smuggled into Wandsworth Prison, and recognised that the phones were being used to instigate escapes and admitted that drugs were being ordered into prison. It was rare for the IMB to have spoken out in this way. In one London prison alone, 250 mobile phones were found during a span of five months.

There are a number of high-profile prisoners who continue to run their criminal activities from behind bars too, according to the Serious Organised Crime Agency. The Government called in an ex-police officer to investigate these matters, but I'm not sure if anything came of it.

In a report carried out by the Prison Service, it admitted that corruption by staff was endemic. It identified seven prisons in England which caused concern: one in Cumbria, two in Kent (which were not identified) and Birmingham, Liverpool, Nottingham and Manchester prisons. The Prison Service and the Metropolitan Police carried out a review and disclosed that their database held information on 3,507 prison staff suspected of wrongdoing. One prison governor freely admitted that he believed there was a corrupt member of staff on each wing to meet the demand from prisoners. Another governor went even further and believed he had 25 corrupt staff and he called his prison the most corrupt in the country.

This is how corrupt prison officers work. They get close to a prisoner who they believe can be trusted and supply him with drugs and mobile phones. The prisoner then sells the drugs on the wing and both officer and prisoner make money. Mobile phones go for different prices in different prisons but can go for as high as £300.

A *Times* newspaper report in April 2008 pointed out that prisoners who sell drugs supplied by prison officers sometimes get jealous of the power of the officer who is supplying the drugs and then grass him up to the decent officers in order to get the officer removed. Prisoners then corrupt other officers to fill the gap.

When the newspaper report appeared, not surprisingly the Government denied the level of corruption within prisons. Maybe the Government would like to explain how £100 million worth of drugs are getting into the prisons? Unlikely from prison visits alone.

A number of the decent prison officers sometimes suspect wrongdoing but are afraid to say anything about the corruption in fear of being isolated and singled-out by their colleagues. If they spoke out their lives would be made unbearable and they could even lose their jobs because of it.

If the Government wants to tackle corruption within prisons it has to have mechanisms in place to protect honest prison officers, and encourage them to come forward with any information. Unless safeguards are put into place to protect those officers, I'm afraid they will continue to keep quiet.

I believe the Prison Service should set up an anticorruption unit with a confidential phone line at its headquarters. Honest prison officers could then report any incidents of corruption, whether it be an officer bringing in drugs and/or mobile phones, without the threat of being isolated and pushed out of their job.

The former Head of the National Offender Management Service, Hussain Djemil, and David Jameson, of the Independent Monitoring Board, agree that most drugs are smuggled in by prison officers. The Government wants to take urgent action on these matters. Many prisoners go into prison having never taken drugs, yet come out with an addiction. I was one of them.

A senior police officer from Merseyside has gone on record and told Government ministers that it is of paramount importance to stop corruption in prisons. He referred to a prisoner who had ordered someone to be shot by using his mobile phone when he was in prison. The victim later died from his injuries.

The Prison Service has stated that it does not tolerate corrupt prison officers. If that is the case, why haven't we seen more prosecutions of corrupt officers? I know of at least two officers who should have been charged and were allowed to leave the service through the back door and get off scot-free.

Nick Herbert, the Minister of State for Policing and Criminal Justice, said: "If prisons are to become places of rehabilitation rather than criminal warehouses, it's essential that corruption is rooted out."

CHAPTER 5

DEATHS IN CUSTODY

DEATHS IN CUSTODY should be a concern to every civilised human being. Since 1990 there have been more than 1,300 deaths in custody. Men, women and children have committed suicide and these deaths could have been prevented if the authorities did their job.

One of those deaths was Alton Manning's, a prisoner who was at a private prison and died of his injuries at the hands of prison officers. Thirty-three-year-old Alton Manning died of asphyxia in December 1995, having been restrained by officers at Blakenhurst Prison near Redditch. A coroner's jury passed a unanimous verdict of unlawful killing. Prison officers were suspended but the Director of Public Prosecutions decided that there was insufficient evidence to bring any criminal charges. After a High Court challenge by Mr Manning's family, the Lord Chief Justice said that the DPP's decision was flawed and should be reconsidered.

In another case prison officers were again at serious fault. Nineteen-year-old Zahid Mubarak of Walthamstow, East London, was attacked just hours before he was due to be released after a 90-day custodial sentence on a dishonesty charge. In a baffling move, prison officers put him in a cell with a known racist called Robert Stewart. Mr Mubarak suffered massive head injuries after being hit at least seven times. He also fractured a forearm and finger after attempting to fend off the blows. He died a week later. Robert Stewart was later convicted of the murder of Mr Mubarak and is doing a life sentence for his crimes.

Mohammed Mudhir is another death the Prison Service could have avoided. At his inquest the jury concluded that Mohammed killed himself while the balance of his mind was disturbed on 21 August 2005. He was on remand at HMP Leeds and was held in cell S1-25 in the segregation unit at the time of his death. The jury listened to the evidence presented in this inquest and reached the following conclusions in their narrative verdict:

> On several occasions healthcare and prison staff were involved with Mohammed and failed to open an Assessment Care in Custody & Teamwork document, commonly known as an ACCT, after evidence would suggest an ACCT be opened, such as lacerations on Mohammed's wrist, strange behaviour and lack of communication. With reference to Prison Service Order 2700 "an act of 'self-harm' is any act where a prisoner deliberately harms themselves..." (see clause 3.1.1) and "An act of 'self-harm' should always be taken seriously..." (see clause 3.1.2). It was felt by the jury that these omissions were in contrast to the guidelines set out in

PSO2700. The jury also felt that failure to open an ACCT could have influenced the circumstances surrounding Mohammed's death.

Multi-disciplinary decision-making was undertaken by healthcare and prison staff in attending Mohammed on the morning of the 18 August 2005 but, due to a lack of communication between Mohammed, prison staff and healthcare staff there was a failure to open an ACCT. Appropriate documentation was also not completed to log this event, i.e. entries in his inmate medical record and prisoner history file. Therefore, this information was not available for other staff when needed.

Indeed, this event was only recorded in the B Wing observation log where the entry read "hostile in presentation, verbalising hatred towards uniform staff. Feels volatile and unable to control himself at times. Not wanting a cellmate as it increases his stress levels. Please be aware of potential for violence and impulsiveness."

The jury felt this could have had a direct influence when prison officers were involved with Mohammed on the evening of the 18 August 2005, when Mohammed displayed aggressive behaviour which was out of character with the behaviour he had previously shown during his time spent in prison.

Mohammed was relocated to the segregation unit on the evening of the 18 August 2005. The segregation staff were unaware of the previous event that had occurred on the morning of the 18 August 2005 regarding the concerns for his mental well-being. There seemed to be no clear procedure for the handover of information resulting in future decisions being taken without the availability of relevant details. Liaison between the duty governor and healthcare staff was imperfect regarding the decision to house Mohammed in the segregation special cell, failing to take into account current circumstances, previous medical or prisoner history. A full medical assessment was not undertaken and the reasons given for this are unacceptable and, therefore, his current mental well-being and potential physical injuries were not established. Mohammed's non-communication was felt to be unhelpful in the assessment of his suitability for segregation.

The jury felt the physical process and procedures for relocation to the segregation special cell using control and restraint techniques were followed correctly. When located in the special cell, the provision of drinking water was overlooked and this was felt to be intolerable, although it was also noted by the jury that Mohammed's failure to communicate and request water contributed to this oversight.

PSO1600 defines the circumstances for continued use of special accommodation and states the prisoner should be regularly monitored so that such use is discontinued immediately when it is no longer necessary. The jury felt this process was not implemented regularly by prison staff and governors, with omissions of reviews resulting in Mohammed spending longer in special accommodation than was necessary. It was also felt that the provision of non-qualified prison staff (operational support grades) overnight as the sole individuals on the segregation unit was inappropriate, offering no opportunity to review Mohammed and move him if this was felt to be suitable. It was also evident that some prison staff assumed he would remain in the special cell overnight regardless of any change in his situation and this was unacceptable. During his time in the special cell, Mohammed was subject to observations every 15 minutes, which is outlined in PSO1600 clause 4.12.5.

The jury felt that the prison staff, including operational support grades, had not received the appropriate training regarding the recording of these observations and the time they occurred. Incidents were not necessarily logged in the appropriate documentation and there seemed inconsistency regarding the use of these documents. Due to these inconsistencies, Mohammed's activities (i.e. drinking/washing from the toilet, excessive praying, restlessness), throughout the time he spent in special accommodation were not highlighted and escalated in the appropriate manner or to the appropriate authority.

On 19 August 2005 Mohammed was visited at 09:24 by the doctor; there were however inconsistencies with the timing of this. The jury felt this review was insufficient and inadequate in order to ensure Mohammed should remain in the special cell. It felt the lack of communication between the segregation prison staff and the doctor and failure to use the inmate medical history hampered the decision-making process. It was also felt that the lack of training for the doctor regarding Prison Service orders was an influencing factor in this process.

The governors gave a consistent view of their

interpretation of Prison Service orders and their expectation of the standard of service to be provided but there was a culture of complacency in the way this service was implemented. Toleration of inadequate practices and the inability to identify and provide appropriate training and support to the staff contributed to the systemic failure. This was evidenced by inconsistent completion of paperwork, failure to communicate clearly their expectations and lack of procedures to regularly monitor the level of service provided by the prison and healthcare staff.

Mohammed was relocated from the special accommodation just before 14:00 on 19 August 2005 into cell S1-25 on the segregation unit. The cells in the segregation unit only accommodate one inmate per cell, yet they had bunk beds in them. The jury felt there was a failure to undertake a thorough risk assessment and, as such, this was something that should have been identified as a potential risk. The beds should have been single, therefore reducing the potential risk of self-harm.

The jury heard evidence that changes have been implemented in the segregation unit at HM Prison, Leeds. These include, but are not limited to: the provision of drinking water in special accommodation; the removal of bunk beds; floor signs identifying which direction is east; aesthetic decorations creating a calmer environment and a mobile library. The jury welcomed these changes that have been implemented in the segregation unit and feel they are a positive improvement.

*   *   *

Prison officers rarely get charged for killing inmates and the system makes excuses when officers are not charged. Manslaughter charges, at the very least, should have been pressed in Alton Manning's case. However, with the system the way it is, I cannot see justice being done in this case or in any other death in custody, due to the lack of will from the Government to do anything about it.

The only redress open to the families of victims is to go to the European Court of Human Rights. Under Article 2 of the Convention on Human Rights, it states quite clearly that everyone has the right to life. I back the family of Alton Manning 100 per cent in their quest for justice in the courts. Prison officers should be held accountable for their actions.

Many prisoners die in prison using what prison officers call the control and restraint method. This should only be used in exceptional circumstances, for example if a prisoner is using violence or is about to use violence against other inmates or prison staff. However, this method is used on a regular basis throughout the prison system. Control and restraint entails violence being used to control the inmate. What the prison officers actually do is bend the wrists back on both hands, causing severe pain to the inmate. They then wrestle the inmate to the floor, put them in a headlock and then handcuff the inmate behind his back.

While this control and restraint method is being applied, it is commonplace for prison officers to punch and kick the inmate while he is on the floor. This is more likely to happen if the inmate had previously assaulted a prison officer – they don't forget things like that and like to get their own back.

Prisoner deaths are often as a result of asphyxia which occurs when inmates are held in a headlock which stops them from breathing. The Home Office and Prison Service banned headlocks many years ago, yet inmates are still being subjected to these headlocks. When prison officers get found out, as in Alton Manning's case, the Prison Service issues statements to the effect that the officers didn't have the proper training; it was a mistake and they are sorry. However, if officers haven't had the proper training, why are they employed by the Prison Service? Inmates are in danger if prison staff are not trained satisfactorily.

The death of women in prisons is also of great concern. The grim pattern to Louise Giles's short life was set at the age of 13 when she took her first overdose. She tried to kill herself throughout her teens, both inside prison, where staff struggled to cope with her acute psychiatric problems, and in the outside world. Three months after being sent to Durham Prison, she was found dead in her cell. She was just 20. The inquest recorded a verdict of accidental death and seriously criticised the regime at Durham Prison.

At the time, the Government made an announcement that they were to expand prisons to cater for the rising prisoner population. But, they put on hold a decision to reform women's prisons, even though the jury in the Louise Giles case raised serious questions as to whether people with mental health problems (such as Louise) were being let down by the system.

Many people believed that the prison authorities were to blame for the death of Louise Giles. The authorities knew of her medical history, including episodes of self-harming, and ignored the warning signs.

Louise Giles self-harmed at least 40 times in New Hall Prison. From the age of 13 she had overdosed at least 20 times. Louise was convicted of murder in 2005 and ended up in Durham Prison's women's unit. On 23 occasions she tried to seriously harm herself because of the frame of mind she was in. Louise was one of only six women in the high-security wing at Durham. The area of the prison where she should have been housed had been closed down some time earlier. Louise's cellmate described her as a small girl with a bubbly type of personality. Louise's cellmate suggested that new staff were inexperienced and tended to "sit on their arses reading *Take a Break* and doing Sudoku". She also thought Louise might have been "pushed over the edge" as the result of an officer slamming her door shut or having no tobacco.

Another prisoner told how staff would take the mickey out of Louise, giving her the nickname 'smelly' as she was not diligent with hygiene. Prison officers had also taken away her radio and television a week before she killed herself.

The jury criticised the prison for not training its staff properly with regard to mental health issues. They went on to say that, because of Louise's condition, the wing in which she was placed was completely unsuitable for her. It condemned the staff for not acting on clear warnings to close the wing, which had been previously recommended in a report.

The jury concluded: "We believe that on the nights leading up to and including the night of Louise's death, she was not appropriately cared for. Signs of emotional distress were overlooked."

Deborah Coles, co-director of the campaign group Inquest, said:

> Louise Giles died as a direct result of the failure of Prison Service officials and ministers to act on the clear warnings that there was a real risk of suicide unless action was taken. Their complacency and inaction is a clear case of corporate manslaughter for which the Prison Service should be brought to account. Punishing women with severe mental problems by incarcerating them in such alienating conditions was cruel, inhuman and degrading treatment.

Shortly after Louise died the unit at Durham was closed down. Louise had been the seventh person to kill herself at this prison in three years.

Prison overcrowding has been blamed for a rise of nearly 40 per cent in prisoners killing themselves. The statistics show that 41 women prisoners have died since 2003 with Lisa Marley, aged just 32, being an example; she died in Styal Prison in 2008.

Figures were released by the Ministry of Justice in 2006 enraged prison reformer campaigners as 67 prisoners had killed themselves. But in 2007 the figure had risen to 92. The statistics also showed that one young offender aged 15 and seven prisoners under 21 had taken their own lives.

But, many prisoners have had their lives saved by prison staff after they attempted suicide. According to ministers, more than 100 prisoners were saved from death.

Government ministers have said that they regret any deaths in custody and everything possible is done to learn the lessons of all these cases. Among the 92 deaths in 2007 were 18 life-sentenced prisoners and 41 prisoners who were awaiting trial, seven women and four prisoners on indeterminate sentences.

The Howard League for Penal Reform's director, Frances Crook, believes that the Prison Service has made huge progress in the prevention of suicides, and blamed a prison crisis for the rise in suicides. I'm not convinced by these arguments at all. Whether prisons are overcrowded or not does not have any bearing on whether someone wants to take their own life, in my opinion. What is significant is the way the suicidal prisoners are treated by the officers and medical staff and, at times, it leaves a lot to be desired.

It's quite commonplace for a prisoner to feel suicidal. When taken into custody, if on a serious charge, like murder, the prisoner does not go to 'normal location' but is taken to the hospital and starts as a Category A prisoner. You are banged up for nearly 23 hours a day, which is enough to make anyone feel suicidal. When I was at Cardiff Prison I self-harmed and was whisked away to the prison hospital, all my clothes were removed from me and

I was placed in a strip cell with just a plastic suit on a mattress on the floor and a chamber pot for a toilet. Can the Prison Service explain to the public how this was going to help me from feeling suicidal? Many prisoners are treated like this at a time when what they need the most is someone to talk to. The experience made me feel more depressed and suicidal, yet no one at the prison gave a damn.

Things got worse for me when a prison officer, who was, I believe, a qualified nurse, told me to pull myself together and then, shockingly, told me that if I wanted to kill myself to make sure that I cut my arm in a certain way and demonstrated how to do it. How many other suicidal prisoners has this officer said this to? He showed a callous and uncaring attitude towards me. What would he have done if I had carried it out and committed suicide? I probably would have just ended up as yet another statistic.

One of the most disturbing cases of suicide has to be the case of Paul Day. He was a police informer and put innocent people in prison. He gave false evidence against Michael Stone who was later convicted of the murder of Lin and Megan Russell. Just before he died, he told his solicitor that he wanted to retract false statements he had made in a series of court cases.

The police are investigating his death and charges may be brought for manslaughter. Paul was coming to the end of his sentence of eight years for robbery when he was found dead in Frankland Prison's segregation unit. At the inquest, the jury heard that Paul had gone on a dirty protest, which means covering your body with excrement, because prisoners and staff were bullying him. They said that he killed himself. But prison officers did nothing to stop the other prisoners from abusing him and there were serious failings in the care towards him.

Andrew and Pauline Day, his parents, complained to the police about the treatment meted out to Paul. An investigating officer on behalf of the Prison Service, Eric Malkin, was appointed to try to find out what had happened. Not surprisingly, this investigation was a total whitewash and the Day family called for an independent inquiry.

The Day family's lawyers made requests for the video tape which showed how prison officers had treated Paul. The authorities said that the tape was no longer in existence. However, after a prisoner had given evidence to say that Paul had been battered badly by the prison officers during the night in question, suddenly video tapes were found. The video tape showed Paul being strip-searched by a number of prison officers in riot suits, and this not long before he died. The ex-governor of the prison, Phil Copple, apologised about the missing tapes and the coroner reacted by stating that it was a glaring admission not to mention the visit of the prison officers that night.

Nearly every time prison officers do something seriously wrong in the segregation units, such as assaults on prisoners, intimidation and other abuses, the Prison Service, on receiving a complaint, covers it up and carries out dishonest investigations and lets prison officers off the hook. Not one prison officer has been charged with manslaughter for the death of Paul Day.

The prison officers who were supposed to protect Paul Day did the complete opposite and were responsible for pushing Paul Day to commit suicide. This, in itself, is a criminal offence. Prison officers clearly broke the law in this case and what they did to Paul was a total abuse of power.

There is now a special team working within prisons to try to prevent prisoners from harming themselves. Jez Spencer and his team are doing all they can and have observed horrific scenes of what prisoners have done to themselves: prisoners cutting their own body parts, setting fire to themselves and even sewing their own lips together.

Jez is also responsible for co-ordinating mental health workers, voluntary groups and prison officers. They all work together to try to spot the prisoners who are at risk of harming themselves. If they become aware of a prisoner who is in danger, they place them on what is described as an assessment, care in custody plan. This allows prisoners to seek the professional help that they need.

While prison officers are actually trained to deal with prisoners harming themselves, I don't think anything can prepare them for the harsh reality of the terrible acts prisoners inflict on themselves and/or others. I have no doubt some officers will be seriously traumatised by what they have seen and will need professional help themselves.

Young offender prisons also have a high rate of self-harm. Thousands of incidents are recorded each year although it is difficult to know how many prisoners are on the assessment, care in custody plan at any one time. Women prisoners are more likely to harm themselves because their children have been taken away from them or maybe because they have been sexually abused and taken drugs. Most prisoners are likely to harm themselves in the first few months of their sentence and are then at their most vulnerable. Prison officers should be on their guard for suicidal prisoners. Sometimes the type of crime committed can take its toll. Life-sentenced prisoners may not be able to cope with the sentence and feel that suicide is the only way out.

Jez Spencer certainly has much to do to reduce the number of suicides in prison. However he and his team have made major inroads in a short space of time. Hopefully resources, time and money for the project are going to be maintained in these dire economic times.

Many of those incarcerated should not be in prison. Some have serious mental health problems and should be in secure hospitals where they can get the specialist help they need. One prisoner, who was on 'normal location' with other prisoners, murdered three prisoners during his time inside. Anyone capable of that has a serious mental illness or is a cold-blooded killer. Yet he was able to walk around the landings as if nothing was untoward and the authorities let him.

Large numbers of prisoners with mental health problems have drugs prescribed to them by the prison doctor to keep them subdued. Take the case of one prisoner I met called Andy who spent most of his time pacing up and down the landings. You walked past him and tried to talk to him, but you were invisible. Andy had a recommendation to serve 30 years before he was considered for parole. The longer you spend in prison, the more likely you are to develop a mental illness. I wasn't ill when I first entered prison, yet I came out with an illness.

Prisons seem to be dumping grounds for mentally ill people. The Government is clueless as to how to deal with them and that seems to suit them. Fifty per cent of female prisoners who have been sentenced suffer from a personality disorder, 63 per cent have neurotic disorders and 14 per cent have psychotic disorders. Seven per cent of men have a psychotic disorder and 40 per cent of male prisoners suffer from neurotic disorders.

The statistics in Scotland fare no better: at least a fifth of prisoners have been put on the suicide risk assessment process. In total 23,420 incidents were recorded in relation to self-harm incidents. Thirty-eight per cent of the prison population have indicated that they have suffered some sort of mental health problems.

One in five male prisoners are prescribed medication such as anti-depressants. The Home Office has actually acknowledged that there are thousands of prisoners who should be transferred to psychiatric units such as Rampton and Ashworth. Why, then, are they being left to rot in the prison system?

Sophie Corslet, from the charity Mind, has stated that prisons are increasingly populated with some of the most vulnerable and socially excluded members of society and that this is having a devastating effect on both individuals and the community as a whole. Mind has argued for years that we need community services which will identify vulnerable people and offer them support well before the point where they are caught up in the criminal justice system. There also needs to be a greater monetary investment into mental health provision within the criminal justice system.

We read in the newspapers all the time of examples of mentally ill people committing serious crimes including murder. The public are then informed that the authorities knew the perpetrator was a danger to the public and had mental health issues, yet nothing was done about it. It's far too late after the event to say we should have done something. More and more prisoners are being released back into our society without getting any psychiatric help and some are, no doubt, a danger to themselves and members of the public. But I also want to stress that not all people with mental illnesses are dangerous and I do not want to tarnish them all with the same brush.

Mentally ill prisoners have a rough time inside; they are taunted by peers and staff alike. It is sickening to think that they cannot defend themselves. This brings me to my ex-brother-in-law, Ellis Sherwood, my co-accused, who recently won £1.4 million for his wrongful conviction. Newspapers ran headlines to say he got this money as compensation for a stroke he suffered after taking drugs while he was in prison. The Prisoners Officers' Association issued a statement condemning the payout. Ellis is in no position to defend himself as he suffered a stroke a couple of years ago. This is the same organisation whose members abused Ellis and me when we were in prison. It seems that they still pick on people who cannot defend themselves, such as Ellis who can hardly speak. They are nothing short of cowards. Their spokesperson, Brian Canton, often cannot get his facts straight. Ellis deserves his compensation. Not one word has come from Brian Canton's mouth to acknowledge that Ellis was an innocent man, or an apology for the way those prison officers treated him.

6

OTHER SIDE OF THE COIN

WHILE I HAVE illustrated a number of things which need addressing within the prison system, it is important to remember that most prison officers are hard-working and dedicated to their jobs. It also must be noted that they have to deal with very dangerous inmates, some with mental problems and some who are just extremely violent. Although I personally didn't get on with prison officers during my time inside, I never once used violence towards them and I don't agree with prisoners using force towards them. I witnessed a number of incidents where prison officers were badly injured having been attacked by prisoners.

Women prison officers are the most vulnerable and are more prone to attacks from prisoners. The past few years have seen significant increases in attacks on women prison officers: examples such as prisoners throwing scalding hot water over them or women officers being stabbed. Many experts have argued that this is down to overcrowding which, in turn, increases the likelihood of offending and has a knock-on effect on rehabilitation programmes. I am not convinced of this argument at all.

Many experts have said that more specialist beds should be made available for mentally ill prisoners who pose a significant risk to themselves and to prison officers. But, as I've already said, mentally ill prisoners should not be within the prison population but in secure mental health hospitals.

The Home Office owes a duty of care to its prison officers and other prisoners. If a mentally ill prisoner seriously injures a prisoner or a prison officer, legal action could be brought against the Home Office for a breach of duty of care for allowing the mentally ill to be on 'normal location' when they should be getting the specialist help they need in a secure hospital.

Since 2000, attacks on women prison officers have risen by 121 per cent, from 232 attacks on women officers in 2000 to 513 in 2006. Assaults on male prison officers have seen a 58 per cent rise. In 2000, the number of attacks were 1,767, but by 2006, 2,804 were recorded. In those six years, the prison population had increased by 24 per cent to record levels.

Frances Crook, director of the Howard League for Penal Reform, said the problems in the Prison Service stemmed from overcrowding and a lack of funds.

"The rise in assaults is absolutely because of the rise in the prison population – not because more prisoners mean more potential assailants, but because pressure of numbers has brought the penal system to its knees," she said.

The Prison Officers' Association spokesperson at the time, Mr Canton, said that attacks on officers had been a factor behind the union's decision to launch wildcat strike action at the time.

"We're not prepared to accept our officers being almost kicked to death on a daily basis," he said. "It's not surprising that officers are miserable when they're scared they might be attacked for doing their jobs."

He accused the Prison Service of being dishonest to the public about its funding, saying: "They need to admit that, if prisons don't get more funding and more officers, we won't be able to search cells for drugs and weapons."

During one incident in 2006 three prison officers were viciously attacked during a day of extreme violence led, allegedly, by the Muslim Boys Gang, al-Qaeda terror suspects at Belmarsh Prison in south-east London. One guard was ambushed by three prisoners and battered with a pool cue and a sock filled with tins of tuna. The incident sparked a riot at the jail's high security unit.

The officer suffered serious head and upper body injuries and needed hospital treatment. As the violence escalated, two other warders were beaten by inmates in the shower block and treatment room. The flare-up came after the *Mirror* newspaper revealed that Belmarsh was run by violent Islamic extremists who were said to be bullying inmates into joining al-Qaeda. A source told the *Mirror*:

The officer is in a pretty bad way. He had some nasty cuts to his head and severe bruising. The prisoners involved have been threatening this for a while. It is the gang's way of trying to make out they run the prison. Things are getting pretty nasty. It's never been this bad before – for three officers to get attacked in one day is very bad. It's a real cause for concern.

The attack came a day after the governor had distributed a memo saying staff enjoyed a cordial relationship with inmates. A total of five prisoners faced disciplinary action over the incidents. The newspaper continued:

The first attack was premeditated. For prisoners to equip themselves with a sock stuffed with tins of tuna and a pool cue shows they meant business. It was a very nasty attack that has shocked even the most experienced staff. Two prisoners who have alleged links to al-Qaeda launched the attack with the weapons. A bystander then joined in for the hell of it. It was frenzied. The officer was hit with the sock and cracked his head on a door as he collapsed. Then they laid into him – he didn't stand a chance. All staff were dispatched to the incident and it ended up with 10 staff and 10 prisoners confronting each other. It was one versus one before the officer was rescued and things calmed down.

According to the newspaper, dogs would normally have been sent in as a first line of response – but the governor ordered that they were not to be used.

The source said: "Officers weren't even allowed to restrain the prisoners to lead them to segregation – which meant they were able to walk unrestrained through the prison after beating up an officer." That would have infuriated the officers, but the governor was more worried about upsetting prisoners due to political correctness. "The prisoners were lording it – and the other inmates were cheering them on."

In the second incident an officer was punched and kicked by an inmate in the shower block in an unprovoked attack. The third assault happened in the treatment room where a warder was beaten after giving a prisoner his medication. The flare-ups came after staff had been ordered to crack down on gangs and bullying.

*   *   *

Sonia Leonard, a prison officer at HMP Wormwood Scrubs, summed up a good day in a BBC news report of April 2006: "If we've managed to get through [the day] without them hurting themselves or anyone else."

"When a man is locked away, he has to ask for everything. He can't go out and do anything, get a toilet roll, help himself," she explains. "There are ten of you, and 250 men, on one wing. Everyone has a need and it's important to make time if they say, 'I need to talk'."

Self-harm, suicide risk and assaults are some of the serious problems the 53-year-old faced at the west London prison.

At the time she had worked there for five years, as a standard grade officer, earning around £26,000 a year. The role is hard, with high sick leave rates because of its physical nature. Cutting is the most common form of self-harm among inmates, although none of the 250 men on Sonia's wing were currently logged in its record book for doing this.

The Scrubs also has one of the highest suicide rates among UK prisons and it was "more and more of a problem", said her fellow officer John Hancock, 55. He believes that the pressure on fewer staff makes it harder to prevent.

Sonia hit the rock bottom of a ten-year career in 2004 when a 29-year-old lifer killed himself. He had about five years left to serve and, as his personal officer, she had to testify at his inquest.

"That's the worst thing I've ever had to do, the lowest point in my career, to go to an inquest and talk about somebody I have done a lot of work with," she said. "When someone kills themselves it's a shock, a terrible experience. You have to go on because it's your job. There are other prisoners to talk to and it affects them."

How to deal with prisoner suicides and their depressive impact among dozens of other inmates, is one of the aspects of weeks of classroom training that officers undergo prior to commencing their jobs. The course also covers control and restraint of prisoners, using the radio, security, how to tackle assault and fighting and their own fitness and dealing with inmates' diversity.

The UK Prison Service had 48,140 staff in 128 prisons in June 2005, (there were another eleven prisons in the private sector). Of those staff nearly half, 24,394, were prison officers. Officers work a 39-hour week, in shifts around the clock, and the job entails many roles: gaoler, counsellor, restrainer.

Each day has a regimented structure – from the counting of inmates at 7.45 a.m., through meals, education, visits, work, and association time, to lock-up at 8 p.m. It is stressful work in a challenging environment. In 2002, the statistics show that there were 2,692 assaults on prison staff. Two years later 1,294 would leave the service, 112 of those on health grounds.

The service's pay review body report for 2006 records that the physical nature of prison work means a higher level of sick leave. But prison officers face more than physical challenges in their daily work. Both Sonia and John testified to the widespread drug use in prison and said that heroin, crack and cannabis had an impact on what they were trying to achieve with inmates.

At Wormwood Scrubs the majority of prisoners have drug and alcohol abuse issues or are in for drug smuggling, as the prison is located near Heathrow and Gatwick airports.

"Drugs come over the prison wall day and night," said John. "If you're not on top of it, it's a problem. There's a huge prison population that uses drugs. If they can't get hold of drugs, the bullying goes up."

Prison officers grapple with an 'amazing' level of illiteracy among prisoners and communication is also an important issue among the increasingly multicultural prison population: currently the Prison Service lacks enough Chinese translators. They also struggle for the funding of staff, resources and courses which harms prisoners' chances for rehabilitation and education.

Given the level of stress and pressures compared to a job outside prison walls, it is a surprise to hear many prison officers describe their work in positive terms.

"Career-wise, it's the best decision I ever made," said Sonia, who added that a previous five-year stint at Feltham Young Offenders' Institution was "wonderful".

"When I applied and was accepted, it was a life-changing moment. I thought I would just have a job for the rest of my life, not a career, but this has opened up so many doors."

She applied to the Prison Service in her 40s after guarding prisoners in court: "I get on well with people. They came to court for a few hours, confided in me and I thought, there must be more I can do. A lot of them had personal troubles, abuse of alcohol or drugs. After 15 to 20 minutes they'd say thank you and I would think 'what have I done?' I'd listened and that made a difference. I'm no soft touch, but everybody – no matter what they've done needs a soft word sometimes."

And John said that he was in the 'right place at the right time' when he decided to join 18 years ago.

"I thought it would be a challenge to be a prison officer because so many different things crop up," he said. "I was good in managing roles with other men. I've seen a little bit of life and the people you come across here don't faze me."

Making prison a workplace has given them a unique perspective. Fresh from jury service on a fraud case, Sonia enjoyed the experience, but not the result. "When we found them guilty, I felt awful. Because I knew where they were going, I knew what it involved, how they would feel."

* * *

Another prison officer who has taken huge pride in his career is Kevin Clift. Interviewed in 2008, he had spent 13 years working in a jail – and he was in no rush to get out. As the principal officer at HMP Littlehey near Huntingdon, Kevin was responsible for the welfare of staff and prisoners one day a week, while carrying out his duties as an orderly officer. His role was as far as it gets from a nine-to-five job – and that's part of its attraction.

Kevin said: "You wear so many different hats. A prison officer can be the parent and the probation officer in one day. You could be dealing with self-harm, restraining someone or telling them about the death of a relative. Then, of course, there are the success stories – prisoners who've been in the system a long time and have turned their lives around, drug addicts who've stayed clean after completing treatment programmes."

Many prisoners have hit rock bottom by the time they get sent to jail. One of the best parts of his job, Kevin said, was seeing ex-offenders fully rehabilitated: "When you've had people at crisis point, to see them go forward is rewarding."

In 1995 Kevin ditched his sales job to become a prison officer, enticed by the variety of opportunities Her Majesty's Prison Service had to offer him.

Kevin said: "I'd always had an interest in prison and police. My father was in the police force and other family members had been in the prison service. It seemed a rewarding job to get into." Before joining the service, he'd worked up to 70 hours a week as a sales representative, racking up 55,000 miles-a-year travelling around the country.

"I thought there was more to life than sitting in a car all day. It was a lonely job."

Working in the Prison Service is anything but – and there's little chance of getting bored or complacent as each day is different. In 1995 Kevin joined HMP Highpoint in Suffolk and was based on an induction and basic regime unit before transferring to HMP Littlehey two years later.

At Littlehey, he started off in a residential wing, helping to run a five-day programme for prisoners with a history of substance abuse. Kevin says: "We were looking at why prisoners take drugs and the effects on family and friends and helping them to break the cycle."

In 2001, Kevin went on to manage the prison's drugs unit. A highly successful programme through the Rehabilitation of Addicted Prisoners Trust (RAPT) was set up and is still running today.

Kevin is so dedicated to that programme that in 2003 he ran a marathon raising £1,800 for RAPT, and added the London Marathon to that achievement in 2010. In 2003 year he was promoted to manage Littlehey's 65 'lifers', i.e. inmates sentenced to life imprisonment.

Kevin progressed to be principal officer for security at Littlehey, overseeing the operational side of the department and dealing with prison intelligence. He was in charge of about 30 staff, including five senior officers. There are numerous opportunities for promotion within the Prison Service.

Kevin said: "If you're prepared to work at it and to travel you can get recognition and rewards."

Housing just over 700 men, Littlehey is situated on the site of the old Gaynes Hall Youth Custody Centre in Perry. It was opened in 1988 as a purpose-built Category C prison, which means its inmates are considered less dangerous and less likely to escape than those in Category A or B jails.

Littlehey's also a trainer prison, with a large emphasis on rehabilitation through education, work and training, including carpentry, car repair, horticulture and catering. Its staff work with partners from the public, private, community and voluntary sectors to offer opportunities for prisoners to develop their skills and attitudes required to make a fresh start.

Prisoners and staff alike take responsibility for ensuring the prison runs smoothly. Littlehey takes a zero tolerance approach to bullying – training inmates in peer support programmes to act as buddies to vulnerable prisoners. A core group of inmates have been trained by the Samaritans to assist and support those 'at risk' prisoners, under a listener scheme.

Kevin said: "If a guy is at crisis point they could spend sometimes hours listening to him."

Staff are trained to deal with all types of situations, including those with the potential to become volatile. Kevin prefers to use his communication skills, rather than force, to diffuse conflicts where possible.

He said: "Staff relations are very good at Littlehey. There's a good sense of working together."

Like many of the staff at Littlehey, Kevin lives

nearby – but never fears for his safety. "A lot of staff live locally without too many concerns. You do get recognised in the street by ex-prisoners. I've had no problems at all. They're probably more embarrassed than you are – especially if they're with their families."

Littlehey offers a huge range of career opportunities, frequently recruiting prison officers, workshop instructors, operational support staff, teachers and catering personnel.

Kevin says anyone considering a prison career should have good interpersonal skills, an open mind and a good sense of humour. "They should have the ability to look at the larger picture, to think before they implement. A sense of humour has got to be a key because it can really diffuse the situation. There is so much banter between staff. Staff also need to be flexible."

*   *   *

Another officer, Pam Chalk, received the Prison Officer of the Year award in 2007 for her work at HMP Wealstun in West Yorkshire. A senior officer, Pam is well respected by colleagues and prisoners.

I spent the day with Pam at her workplace and saw examples of how she helps prisoners from day-to-day. She's hardly through the security gate when a prisoner in his early 30s, waiting for a taxi to take him to a job interview, stops her to talk about his lack of prospects.

"Don't be disheartened," she says.

"I can't help being disheartened, I'm only human. I've never had a job. I've got 160 previous. I've been in jail all my life," he replies.

She tells him she'll speak to one of the resettlement staff about a placement. Afterwards she adds: "He's applied for 90 jobs. He wants to work, but he's a prolific offender and no one wants him. Sometimes we turn people out with £50 in their pocket, but how can you live on that? You need a job."

It's the same throughout Pam's shift. Prisoners stop her to chat about something she's chasing up for them, or just to say how she's helped them.

One says: "She will help anyone who needs helping, as long as it's sensible. She'll get on with it and you know she'll follow it through." Another describes how she arranged a home visit, so that he could visit his mother who was dying of cancer.

Pam runs the prisons listeners' scheme which provides volunteers, trained by the Samaritans, who sit down for confidential chats with those people who need to share their problems. The prisoner co-ordinator values Pam's guidance and says his team of listeners help tackle bullying and self-harm, adding: "Someone might have had a bad visit from a girlfriend, or made a phone call to someone in hospital. Problems here can seem a lot more serious because we can't do much about them."

Pam's manager was Principal Officer Bill Hosie, recently transferred to Yorkshire from HMP Highpoint in Suffolk. He said of Pam: "She certainly justifies the award. She always goes the extra mile."

During her decade at HMP Wealstun, Pam has

worked on the 'open' side, but was currently on the 'closed' side as the senior officer for B Wing, in charge of a team of six which looks after 159 prisoners.

Her shift began at midday and she spends the first hour on paperwork. Later, she helps supervise the line route, a busy half-hour when most prisoners leave their cells to walk to workplaces within the prison, such as the laundry or gardens, or attend courses such as bricklaying, catering and artwork.

Her team also chases up people who should be working, but aren't. "Most of them like to go to work, but there's always the odd one who doesn't want to do anything. If someone doesn't go, I give them my 'career talk' in the office."

Prisoners on B wing have a strong incentive to co-operate because they enjoy enhanced privileges that new arrivals don't, such as more time to mix with other prisoners, snooker tables and watching DVDs at weekends.

"If they get two warnings I get them in and tell it how it is, and they know it might mean leaving the wing. In my experience, 99 per cent toe the line. They realise what they'll lose," says Pam. When the prisoners walk back to their cells, at around 4 p.m., she helps supervise the route again before they are served their evening meal at around 5.30 p.m. She never knows what drama might erupt on a particular day. "You'll see someone with a black eye, and that can take up a lot of time making inquiries," she says.

"When we have to tell a prisoner that someone has died, I really feel for them because they can't be with their families, or when they get a 'dear John' letter, because someone has ended a relationship. I've had people in the office in floods of tears," she says, brandishing a toilet roll that sits on her desk, adding: "I think they like talking to me because I'm a bit older. People in here have a lot of issues such as family problems, or child abuse. If someone goes out of here with a job and meets someone and does all the family stuff, or comes off drugs, then that is a success."

*   *   *

Jim Dawkins is an ex-prison officer who has worked at Belmarsh, Wormwood Scrubs and Wandsworth Prisons in London. He has written two books about prison life and took part in Channel 5's television series, *Banged Up*. On the Crimestoppers website he gave an account of what it was like being a prison officer:

> During my time as a prison officer, I found some glaring flaws with the system which I did not agree with, and which ultimately led to my decision to leave the service prematurely in 1999. I documented my experiences in my book, *The Loose Screw*, in which I made a point of being quite brutally honest about what I witnessed and how I felt the system was being managed. I am totally in favour of the need for prisons and custodial sentences for criminals and have no regard for anyone who commits crime of any sort. However, I know first-hand that there are some serious problems in the current prison system, which needs to be addressed with immediate effect.
>
> The initial flaws of the prison system stem from the bad apples among a minority of staff, who spend their

days bullying and assaulting prisoners and putting other, more junior staff, under immense pressure to do the same. Some people have the opinion that it's part of the process that prisoners should have a hard time while they're inside, but staff bullying has a negative effect and does not help criminals to see the error of their wrongdoing. As a prison officer, you are employed to protect the public by keeping those committed by the courts in custody, and to help them to lead law-abiding lives on their release. You are given absolute power over the prisoners, as you control every move. The problem with power is that it can often go hand-in-hand with corruption. Although members of staff who participate in these acts are in a minority, they do cause incredible strain on other officers and prisoners who are just trying to do a difficult job well, or get through their sentence, learn to understand the consequences of their actions, and change their behaviour for their release back into our society.

The most important job as a prison officer is to act as a role model for the prisoners under your care and to show them the errors of their ways. Those officers who walk the prison landings, like predatory animals, build reputations of preying on weaker prisoners, and assault prisoners in unprovoked attacks, are not teaching inmates that breaking the law is wrong and will not be tolerated in our society. I've also known prison officers to have planted contraband in cells and smuggle contraband into prison, for a price of course. These acts breed a vicious contempt between prisoners and staff and prison ultimately becomes a battle ground for survival. Furthermore, prisoners end up leaving prison with nothing but resentment and more often bitterness and hatred for authority than they entered with.

Prisoners were afraid to sleep on the first night and some could not sleep at all as they were terrified that their cell mate might physically or even sexually assault them. They would not describe the hours of mind-numbing boredom when, due to lack of staff or an incident, they were locked up in a cell measuring four foot by eight foot. It is these stories that young people need to hear before they find themselves in a prison van at the start of a five-year sentence or worse. Young people also need to feel some pride in their communities, in the hope that they will learn not to destroy property or rob the elderly or become involved in futile gang fights where no one wins, but lives get destroyed. But just as prison officers have to be role models to inmates, adults also have an obligation to behave as role models for young people to look up to and respect in their communities. Perhaps if more of us pulled together to try to do more to encourage these young people to channel their energies into getting some community pride and spirit back, and if we earn their respect instead of taking every opportunity to chastise them, we may be able to deter these young people from a life of crime. In turn, the problem of overcrowding in our prisons would naturally be tackled too. Furthermore, tackling poverty in the community would, in my view, also help to reduce crime. It's a proven fact that the kind of people who end up in prison can be attributed to their poor social background. How many millionaires do you see in prison for breaking the law?

Many young people really believe that crime pays, but I have yet to meet a person who has been involved in a life of crime who would not swap the measly amounts of money they may have made for the chance to have the years back that they wasted in prison. Getting this message across to our young people is the key. They need to hear first-hand from people who have experienced the grim reality of being locked up for years, or how it feels to be a victim of crime and to reach the source of prison overcrowding. We need to work on our communities to bring back the community spirit I remember when I was growing up, so that we no longer fear attack every time we leave our homes.

* * *

The key role of prison officers in cutting re-offending is undermined by a crisis in the prison system say MPs. In a report released recently in 2009, 'The Role of the Prison Officer', the House of Commons justice committee said that the positive work done by uniformed prison officers was undermined by a crisis in the prison system and would be further threatened by planned changes. The result will be more victims, more crime, more fear of crime, and poor value from an already very costly prison system.

Justice committee chairman, Sir Alan Beith MP, said:

> Prison officers are undervalued, and their contribution to making ex-prisoners less likely to commit crimes is constantly undermined. It is the uniformed prison officer who is often the only positive role model a prisoner sees. Good officers use their skills and experience to build constructive relationships with prisoners so as to maintain security and to encourage them to change their lives. This becomes impossible when prisons are overcrowded, staff time with inmates is cut and prisoners are constantly shunted around between different prisons. Prison officers in England and Wales also receive far less training than their counterparts in many other countries and officers get fewer opportunities to develop their education than prisoners. Efficiency savings, some aspects of the Workforce Modernisation Programme and the proposed 1500-place prisons all look like making things far worse.

Despite a rising prison population, the Ministry of Justice is required to make savings of approximately £900 million by the end of 2011. Half of the ministry's budget is for the new National Offender Management Service (NOMS). Half of the NOMS budget is for prisons and 72 per cent of the Prison Service's budget goes on staff. It seems inevitable, therefore, that the Ministry of Justice is looking for a significant cut in funding for prison officers, further reducing the ratio of prison officers to prisoners. This is a change the committee says will damage efforts to reduce re-offending rates over the longer term.

Evidence to the committee highlighted the potential that prison officers have to challenge prisoners' offending behaviour but also the difficulties that prison officers face in trying to have a positive impact in the current prison system. The first problem identified by the MPs is the short training course provided for new recruits, who may be as young as 18 years old, which is supposed to equip them to deal with a very wide range of offenders in prison. Added to this, the committee says that overcrowding, staff shortages and the high proportion of prisoners with unaddressed mental health, drug or alcohol problems, means that the system is constantly at crisis point. This leaves little or no time to build productive relationships with prisoners which are crucial, not only for rehabilitation, but also for maintaining mutual respect and, ultimately, good order and security in prisons. This also limits the resources available for effective on-the-job training or mentoring to fill gaps in the knowledge and skills of new officers.

While the number of prisoners has spiralled, there has not been a corresponding increase in the number of prison officers. In total 24,272 uniformed officers were employed throughout the prison estate in 2000, rising to 26,474 by the beginning of 2006, an increase of nine per cent. As already mentioned, over the same period, the prison population has increased by 24 per cent. The committee also said that the Government's policies on 1,500-place prisons, clustering and prison workforce modernisation were likely to further de-skill the prison officer's role to that of a turnkey.

The implications of the Government's prison workforce modernisation programme for staff and managers run counter to much of the evidence the committee heard on what would make a strong and effective Prison Service.

Technology, such as cameras and automated locking, cannot replace the positive example-setting, engagement and the challenging of prisoners behaviour which are the most valuable parts of the prison officer's role. The committee said the workforce modernisation programme, as currently proposed, represented a missed opportunity to develop the right Prison Service for the twenty-first century.

Sir Alan concluded:

> The evidence we have received over several inquiries, in particular via the e-consultations we have run, suggests strongly that prison officers have a core contribution to make to the rehabilitation of offenders, which they themselves recognise and are proud of. To avoid prison being 'an expensive way of making bad people worse' we need to maximise the influence of such officers, and other

prison staff, over whether a particular offender goes on
achieve a law-abiding lifestyle. Proper training, on-the-job
support from senior colleagues and, at the end of the day,
more time to work with prisoners are all vital elements
in this. There are resource implications for governors but
the long-term payback will be significant.

7

PRISONERS FOR LIFE

THERE ARE TWO different categories of life sentences: a mandatory life sentence, where the trial judge has no option but to pass a life sentence as in the case of murder, and a discretionary life sentence, where the trial judge can, if he thinks the offence is serious enough, pass a life sentence or give the convicted person a fixed prison term. A discretionary life sentence is given to those convicted of manslaughter or arson and those persistent offenders who commit crimes of robbery.

Once a prisoner has been given a life sentence, whether it is a mandatory or discretionary, the trial judge has to make some sort of recommendation to the Home Office as to the minimum time that person has to serve before he or she is eligible for parole and possible release. This, however, has brought the judiciary and the Home Office into considerable conflict with each other on many occasions. There are currently 33 prisoners serving a whole life tariff in England and Wales. Among the most notorious on that list are:

The longest serving is **Ian Brady**, one of the Moors murderers, who was given two life sentences in 1966 for the murders of Lesley-Ann Downey, 10, John Kilbride, 12, and Edward Evans, 17. The body of 16-year-old Pauline Reade, another victim, was discovered on Saddleworth Moor in 1987. Brady went on a hunger strike for a year demanding the right to die. Judges ruled a couple of years ago, in 2000, that the authorities at Ashworth Special Hospital were right to force feed him to keep him alive. He is still serving his time and will never be released. His partner in crime, Myra Hindley, was sentenced to 25 years in 1966 for her part in the murders of Downey and Kilbride. She later confessed to killing Pauline Reade and Keith Bennett. Hindley later died of cancer in prison.

Peter Moore, 69, dubbed the 'Man in Black', murdered four men in Wales in 1995. During his trial, Moore, who owned and managed a chain of cinemas in north Wales, told the jury the crimes were committed by a homosexual lover he nicknamed Jason after the killer in the 'Friday the 13th' horror films. The jury found him guilty on all counts.

Malcolm Green was given a life sentence in 1971 for killing a prostitute, and was released after serving 18 years. Five months later in 1990, he killed, apparently without motive, a tourist from New Zealand whom he had befriended. He dismembered the body and dumped it in plastic bags, at several spots along a road in south Wales. He was jailed for life again.

Jeremy Bamber was given five life sentences in 1986 for shooting his adoptive parents, his sister and her twin sons in order to gain a £500,000 inheritance. In 1995 he lost an appeal against the then Home Secretary's ruling that he should never be released. To this day, he continues to protest his innocence and is actively trying to get the conviction overturned. I hope he does, because I believe he did not commit the crime.

John Duffy, the so-called 'railway killer', was given seven life sentences in 1988 for two murders and three rapes between 1975 and 1986. He gained his nickname after stalking his victims to remote train stations before attacking them. In 1999 he admitted another 17 further sex offences.

The civil servant, **Dennis Nilsen**, was jailed for life in 1983 for killing six gay men. He picked up rent boys and homeless men at gay clubs in Soho, strangling them and keeping the bodies in his bedroom, sometimes sketching them or having sex with the corpses. He was caught when the drains at his north London house became blocked with body parts.

Victor Miller, a computer operator, indecently assaulted and murdered a 14-year-old boy after abducting him on his paper round in Hagley, Worcestershire, in 1988. Police believe he may have carried out 28 further sexual assaults. It was only after being arrested for another attack that Miller led police to the boy's battered body, hidden under a pile of leaves. The court heard that he preyed on paperboys because they were particularly vulnerable. He has requested to remain in prison for the rest of his life.

Rosemary West was given ten life sentences in November 1995 for helping her husband Fred rape, torture and kill young women at their home in Gloucester. He had admitted 12 murders, but hanged himself in prison while awaiting trial. Among the victims was West's daughter, Heather, her step-daughter Charmaine, and a woman pregnant by Fred West.

Arthur Hutchinson was a petty criminal who had a history of violence. He gatecrashed a wedding reception at the home of a Sheffield solicitor in 1983 and stabbed to death the bride's mother, father and brother, before raping her sister at knifepoint. A palm print on a bottle of champagne helped lead police to him. He was jailed for life in 1984.

Victor Castigador was an illegal immigrant who came to Britain from the Philippines in 1985. Castigador was jailed for life in 1990 for murdering two Sri Lankan security guards during a robbery at a Soho amusement arcade where he also worked. Along with two other men, he tied the guards and a female cashier up, doused them in white spirit and locked them in a wire cage in the basement before tossing in lit matches.

The so-called 'Beast of Manchester', **Trevor Hardy**, 63, murdered three teenage girls in the city in the 1970s.

Robert Maudsley, 56, has killed three fellow prisoners while serving time for a murder he committed in 1974.

Would-be serial killer **Mark Martin**, 29, killed three women before his capture put an end to his ambitions.

Andrezej Kunowski, 52, murdered a 12-year-old girl in her home. Dubbed 'The Beast', he had already been found guilty of 27 sexual offences in his native Poland.

Hitman **Paul Glen**, 36, was jailed for his second murder in 2005. He stabbed the wrong victim.

*   *   *

These men and women have all received mandatory life sentences. The Home Secretary has the power to release them on licence at any time, but he or she is under no obligation to do so or to refer their cases to or accept recommendations from the Parole Board, the body which advises on the release of prisoners. These men and women are serving whole life tariffs. Politicians have decided that life, in each of these cases, really does mean life. And that stance was recently upheld when Jeremy Bamber and two other convicted murderers lost their appeal to the European Court of Human Rights that whole-life tariffs condemning prisoners to die in jail amounted to 'inhuman or degrading treatment'.

Even at this level, the whole life tariff seems remarkably unfair and open to abuse. Without doubt those who are a danger to the public should be imprisoned. But it is also wrong that the hope of a release at some point is also extinguished for these lifers.

One high profile case, which has brought the judiciary and the Home Office into serious conflict, has been the case of the Bulger killers. Robert Thompson and Jon Venables were convicted of killing James Bulger, a toddler. They were only ten years old at the time of the offence.

Michael Howard was in charge of the Home Office when Venables and Thompson were found guilty of murder. He tried to increase their sentences from eight to 15 years. This was contrary to what the trial judge recommended. A challenge to the courts was inevitable, and Lord Woolf quashed the 15-year tariff Michael Howard had imposed and substituted it with eight years in conjunction with the trial judge's recommendations.

I believe the judges got it wrong in this particular case – 15 years, because of the nature of this crime, should have stood. However, I do believe that, on the whole, judges do get it right when setting life-sentence prisoners' tariffs, mainly because the politics are taken out of the decision-making process. The Home Secretary has too many outside influences to make a just decision on life-sentenced prisoners' tariffs.

For example, the reporting in the newspapers of a particular crime can influence the Home Secretary to increase a prisoner's tariff.

In those cases where the innocent protest their conviction, many are denied parole on the basis that they have not addressed their offending behaviour and are therefore a high risk to the public. I know of only three cases where those protesting their innocence have actually achieved parole. Dr Michael Naughton, an academic at Bristol University, has written extensively on the issue of the 'parole deal' in relation to prisoners maintaining their innocence. The Parole Board denies that the parole deal exists. I can confirm that the parole deal does exist. I was informed by those in authority that if I didn't address my offending and admit my guilt I would never be released. Prisoners who are fighting to prove their innocence are regularly told by the prison psychiatrists, prison officers and probation officers that they will never be released if they don't admit their guilt.

Every prisoner who protests their innocence knows that unless they get their names cleared at the Appeal Courts, they probably will never be released.

The system cannot cope with innocent prisoners and they get singled out for oppressive treatment by the authorities. I wrote to the Home Office on numerous occasions, but no one ever replied or did anything about the way I was being treated. As I write this book, you can be sure of one thing, some other prisoner in the system is having the same treatment meted out to him that I had, all because of the fact that he is innocent and shouldn't be there.

8

PRISONERS' RIGHTS

PRISONERS RETAIN CERTAIN basic rights which survive despite imprisonment. The rights of access to the courts and of respect for one's bodily integrity (that is, not to be assaulted) are fundamental rights of this sort. Prisoners can only lose those civil rights either expressly by an Act of Parliament or by 'necessary implication', in other words as a consequence of some other law under which the action is being taken.

The state is allowed to place limits on prisoners' rights if it is considered necessary for the prevention of crime, prison security or to protect the safety of the prisoner or others. Any limitations placed upon such rights must be proportionate to the aim that the authorities are seeking to achieve. A large number of cases have been heard by the European Court on Human Rights on principles such as the right to marry, the right to family life, the right not to be tortured and access to journalists – and this has helped to clarify the extent to which limitations can be imposed.

Many prisoners are constantly told by prison officers that they do not have any rights and that *they* are the law. I have heard this on many occasions, but it is a complete myth. There have been a number of judicial reviews brought by prisoners over the years to try and establish prisoners' rights.

They range from the right to marry while in prison, to access to journalists. Some important cases have been decided in favour of prisoners. One of the earliest cases was *Hamer* v. *UK* 1983. Hamer wanted to marry his partner while he was in prison and asked the governor for permission to do so. The governor refused his request and Hamer started High Court proceedings. Hamer lost his case in the High Court, Appeal Court and the House of Lords. However, all was not lost and Hamer asked the European Court of Human Rights to hear his arguments and he was successful. The Government then brought in the Marriage Act 1983 to comply with the ruling and Hamer later married.

Another important case to come before the European courts was *Campbell and Fell* v. *UK* 1984. This referred to letters sent to solicitors which contained allegations of prison abuse – the prison governor was able to read letters and stopped them from being posted out to solicitors. This was on the grounds that they had to air their grievances with the prison authorities first. Campbell and Fell went through the same procedures as Hamer, achieving no success until their cases came before the European Court of Human Rights. The court ruled that their case was a violation of Articles 8 and 10 of the Convention on Human Rights.

The most important case for prisoners' rights came about at the House of Lords in *Raymond* v. *Honey* 1983, where the courts ruled that prisoners maintain all their civil rights in prison unless Parliament has expressly taken them away. This was a landmark ruling and meant that unless Parliament had taken away prisoners' rights by legislation, the Prison Service could not do so either.

However, the Prison Service and governors of prisons are a law unto themselves and ignore the law if they don't like a certain right that a prisoner has, and they deliberately put obstacles in the way. If the prisoner tries to exercise his right, prison officers step in and harass the prisoner by interfering with his mail, using bullying tactics and sometimes even resorting to violence.

The other trick the Prison Service and prison governors use against a prisoner, especially if he challenges their unlawful decision in the courts, is to transfer the prisoner as far away as possible from his family so that he cannot get visits from them, isolating the prisoner from everybody in the process.

The Prison Service and the governors of prisons are very vindictive against any prisoner who dares to challenge them in the courts and there are always repercussions by them against the prisoner. I've been on the receiving end of such revengefulness and suffered a backlash for fighting for what is right when I was in prison. Prisoners who are brave enough to stand up for their rights need to know that they will be in for a rough ride from the system. These practices need to be exposed because it is illegal to behave in that manner. I hope this book in some small way does just that.

Under the European Convention on Human Rights people have a right to start a family and it would be interesting to know whether this applies to prisoners. Of course, this has never been argued before the courts but in my view should be challenged. Why should the partner of a prisoner and someone who has committed no criminal offence be denied the right to start a family? The wife, in effect, would be punished for the crimes of her husband which, in my view, is unlawful and it could be argued that she is being punished through no fault of her own.

One area of concern to me, which I mentioned earlier, is the illegal practice of making prisoners squat during cell searches and after visits from family. While strip-searching of prisoners is a necessary evil, the Prison Service and prison officers cannot justify asking prisoners to bend over with no pants on so that they can look at anal passages to see if they are concealing drugs. They cannot justify the violence used by prison officers if a prisoner refuses to squat as it falls within the definition of inhuman and degrading treatment. Yet violence was carried out on prisoners who refused to comply on a regular basis when I was in prisons. This is another area which needs to be challenged through the courts.

Some significant changes have come about in relation to prison law after prisoners challenged rulings in the courts. John Hurst won a case, in relation to prisoners speaking to the media via telephone, at the Court of Human Rights. John Hurst also brought a case before the same court in 2005 with regard to the right of prisoners to vote. The court stated that there was no justification for the UK Government to stop prisoners from voting. More than six years later, the Government still has not implemented the right of prisoners to vote and if the policy is not in place by the next general election, that election will be null and void. It remains to be seen whether the Government will implement the new legislation or water it down. We will have to wait and see how this matter unfolds with time.

9

THE CCRC AND THE INNOCENCE PROJECT

THE CRIMINAL CASES Review Commission (CCRC) was set up in 1997 in the wake of a Royal Commission report into one of the biggest cases of miscarriage of justice, the Birmingham Six. It was recognised that there were potentially many other miscarriage of justice victims languishing in prison and their plight needed addressing. The CCRC was given wide-ranging powers to investigate wrongful convictions and made great progress in its first year.

My case was one of the first to be referred to the Court of Appeal and I later proved my innocence, thanks to the hard work of the CCRC. It enlisted an expert in order to establish that my co-accused was a 'Walter Mitty character', prone to fantasising. It also called in an outside police force which later established that the police in the original investigation had not told the truth etc. – the list is endless. However, that was nearly 11 years ago but things have now, unfortunately, changed.

These days, in order to refer a case back to the Court of Appeal, the CCRC applies a 'real possibility' test. After re-evaluating the evidence in the case, if the CCRC isn't confident that the Court of Appeal will overturn the conviction (even if it thinks the person is innocent), the case will not be sent back to the court. The CCRC is now, in effect, second-guessing what the Court of Appeal might do, acting as judge and jury.

This is now very unfair. It's up to the Court of Appeal to decide the merits of the case and *not* the CCRC. Moreover, the CCRC will not consider evidence if it was available at the trial and was not used by the defence, even if it changes the whole picture of what happened. I am of the view that any evidence which changes the circumstances of the allegation and points to a person's innocence must be considered – yet the CCRC will not do so, and this causes further injustice. Since its inception, it's sad to say that the organisation has changed beyond all recognition. It hardly ever investigates miscarriages of justice unless they are handed to it on a plate by solicitors doing all the work and finding new evidence. This should also be the job of the CCRC, because that's what it was set up to do – investigate – yet it rarely does.

The CCRC has stated that it is underfunded, staff are demoralised, and that this hampers what it can do to help the innocent. However, the CCRC has a big voice and can speak out in the media about what is going on, yet, more often than not, it refuses to say anything. The CCRC, in my view, is a spent force and, because of this, many other onlookers feel the same.

This disaffection with the commission has led to the Innocence Project, which was the brainchild of Dr Michael Naughton of Bristol University. He felt that the CCRC was not doing enough to help miscarriage of justice victims. His organisation exists to raise public awareness of wrongful convictions. It undertakes research that identifies the causes of miscarriages of justice, legal reform and encourages the establishment of other Innocence Projects in the UK.

In response to public concerns about wrongful convictions, the Government's White Paper, *Justice For All*, in 2001 stated that it had an 'absolute determination to acquit the innocent'. But, our system of justice is not about the objective truth of a suspect, or a defendant's guilt or innocence. Adversarial justice is a contest, regulated by principles of due process, compliance with the rules and procedures of the legal system. During the legal process errors can be made and forms of malpractice can occur, with the result that some innocent people will be wrongly convicted and some guilty offenders will be acquitted.

Dr Naughton believes that the CCRC, the body set up in the wake of notorious cases such as the Guildford Four and the Birmingham Six, was *not* designed to rectify the errors of the system and to ensure that wrongful convictions were overturned. Instead, its remit under the 1995 Criminal Appeal Act dictates that it reviews the cases of alleged or suspected victims of a miscarriage of justice to test whether they were obtained in strict accordance with the rules and procedures of the system.

If it is found that the procedures of the criminal justice system process were contravened and that there was a real possibility that the Court of Appeal would overturn the conviction, the case would be referred back to the Court of Appeal.

Dr Naughton goes on to say that the CCRC will refer the cases of guilty offenders if their convictions were procedurally incorrect. At the same time, it is often helpless to refer the cases of innocent victims of wrongful convictions if they do not meet the required criteria of fresh evidence or fresh arguments.

The Innocence Project's launch at Bristol University's School of Law on the 3 September 2004 attracted prominent academics, leading activists, interested parties from campaigning organisations and criminal appeal lawyers from the UK, USA and Australia. At least 25 universities across Britain have since set up Innocence Projects, including Cardiff, which is significant considering the amount of Welsh cases of injustice over the past 20 years. Julie Price, who runs the Innocence Project at Cardiff, has been instrumental in raising awareness of miscarriages of justice, and works closely with Dr Naughton.

Innocence Project volunteers work on live cases where they believe there has been a miscarriage of justice. Law students are allocated a case to work on with supervision from a qualified lawyer. They try to seek avenues which were previously overlooked or where there may be new leads or new evidence. If they do find evidence they then prepare a case to be put forward to the CCRC in the hope of the case being referred back to the Court of Appeal. This is a time-consuming process and the work of investigating these cases is colossal, and students bear the brunt of the case. The Innocence Project has had success in referring cases to the Court of Appeal.

The Innocence Project is going from strength to strength and can only benefit the thousands of prisoners who are languishing in prisons all over the country. It's a fresh avenue for those claiming their innocence. But, there are criteria which have to be followed before the project can look at a case. Prisoners need to write to the Innocence Project setting out their case as best they can. A completed questionnaire will then help the Innocence Project to get a clearer picture of the case to see if it needs more information. The Innocence Project only deals with factual innocence, not technicalities, and has *no* desire to help the guilty.

If, on the other hand, the project decides a case is worth pursuing, everything will be done to try to assist the wrongly convicted person and no stone will be left unturned to get at the truth.

10

THE TREATMENT OF WELSH PRISONERS

WELSH PRISONERS AND their families get a very rough deal in relation to the prison system. More often than not, Welsh prisoners with lengthy sentences are shipped out to English prisons away from their loved ones

This problem could easily be resolved by the authorities if they built more prisons in Wales for men and women. However, a proposal to build a prison in north Wales was blocked. You have to ask, why? Prisons in Wales are badly needed and the families of the prisoners are being punished, yet they haven't committed an offence. Home Office policy states that prisoners should be kept near their families.

Following the decision of the Ministry of Justice to withdraw its interest in building a new prison at the former Dynamex site near Caernarfon in north Wales, the Welsh Affairs Committee announced that it would conduct a follow-up inquiry to its 2007 report, *Welsh Prisoners in the Prison Estate*. The Committee issued a call for new written evidence from any interested parties on recent developments affecting the prison estate in Wales.

The chairman of the committee, Dr Hywel Francis MP, said:

> The committee had warmly welcomed the Government's decision to build a new prison near Caernarfon. Following the announcement by the Ministry of Justice that there may now be specific problems with the Dynamex site, the Welsh Affairs Committee recognises that there is a vital need to revisit the issue of Welsh prisoners in Wales. We hope that the Government will still acknowledge that there is an urgent need for prison facilities in north Wales.

The 2007 report recommended that more prisons needed to be built in Wales to combat the pressures of overcrowding and to enable prisoners to be held closer to home. The report had been a response to the fact that nearly half of Welsh prisoners were incarcerated outside Wales. Currently there are only four prisons in Wales, all of which are in south Wales, and there is no prison for women in the country at all.

Welsh prisoners are treated like dirt. At English prisons, prison officers regularly call them 'sheep shaggers', 'taffy' and accuse the Welsh of being thick. These very offensive words were used against me in nearly all the prisons I found myself in. If you had the balls to put in a complaint against the officers, your life would be made hell. Not many prisoners would complain for fear of reprisals. I personally didn't give a damn and said it how it was, whether they liked it or not. I used to let most of it go over my head but I would be a liar if I said it didn't get to me, because it did.

One day, I had a right go at the officers and said that we might shag the sheep but you eat them afterwards. That didn't go down too well with the officers, and I was surprised they didn't do anything to me. It bugs me that Welsh people are the butt of racial jokes and that the law does not protect us under the Racial Discrimination Act 1997. I believe the law should be changed to include the Welsh under this Act. Maybe this will be another campaign for me to take up in the future.

There should be at least another six prisons built in Wales to accommodate the number of Welsh prisoners being sent to prison and to bring home Welsh prisoners from English prisons. Statistics compiled by the Home Office show that prisoners who maintain regular contact with their families are less likely to commit further offences. There should be two women's prisons in Wales. Welsh women prisoners end up in either East Wood Park or Holloway in England. Both prisons are inadequate to deal with the needs of Welsh women.

In 2006, Jenny Willott, Liberal Democrat MP for Cardiff Central, raised the issue of Welsh women in prison saying:

Female Welsh offenders are all held in prisons in England. This means that their partners and children may have to set aside entire days to travel hundreds of miles to see them. My concern is this: mothers deserve access to their children and children need to be able to see their mothers regularly. Keeping families so far apart is very damaging to the welfare of the family and is likely to increase the chances of offending behaviour amongst the children of female prisoners, and decrease the mother's chances of successful rehabilitation. I am determined to push for facilities for female prisoners in Wales as part of the Government's prison review. Welsh families must not be damaged by the imprisonment of a mother many hundreds of miles from her children.

More than five years later nothing has been done in relation to the issues raised by Jenny. It is obvious that the Government does not give a damn about Welsh prisoners and that they are low on their list of priorities.

The need for Welsh prisons has become so desperate that the police are having to baby-sit Welsh prisoners in police cells. Welsh Liberal Democrat research has revealed that police forces in Wales have been forced to house nearly 3,500 prisoners in their police cells due to prison overcrowding, at a cost of more than £3.2 million – the equivalent of more than 100 extra police officers.

The figures contained in a Freedom of Information request and parliamentary questions from Jenny show that the average cost of housing a prisoner in a police cell in Wales is £942 per night – two and a half times Government estimates and twelve times the cost of housing them in prison.

Commenting, Jenny said:

The Government's prisons crisis is forcing our police to baby-sit thousands of Welsh prisoners rather than catching criminals, and leaving the taxpayer to pick up the rocketing bill. Labour has massively underestimated the knock-on costs of their mismanagement of the criminal justice system. If this £3.2m of public money was spent sensibly, we could have over 100 extra police officers on the streets of Wales. Instead, money is pouring down the drain as prisons are packed to bursting. The police have to take the spill over, and the vast majority of offenders never get the drug, alcohol or mental health treatment they need to solve many of the problems behind their crimes. The Government has put us in this hopeless position by failing to plan for the future while putting record numbers behind bars in an effort to appear tough on crime. Meanwhile, reoffending levels remain the highest in Western Europe.

I agree with Jenny that urgent action is needed so that prisons are built in Wales sooner rather than later. My own experiences of being in prison have also shown that, if you are Welsh and seen as a problematic prisoner fighting for your rights, you will be taken to a prison so far away from your family that it is nearly impossible for them to visit. I ended up in Frankland Prison, not far from Newcastle, and all because I took the prison governor to court. I'm not the first that this has happened to and I won't be the last but this practice has to stop. Most prisoners call this ghosting. If I had been at a Welsh prison, would this have happened? I doubt it.

A Welsh Affairs Select Committee report in 2007 echoes many of my concerns:

> The Welsh Affairs Select Committee decided to undertake this inquiry in order to address concerns about the imprisonment of Welsh prisoners in prisons outside of Wales, in many cases a long way from homes. The Government is planning to create 8,000 new prison places by 2012, including some in Wales, and it is therefore

timely to examine provision in Wales. We believe that the devolution of powers to the National Assembly for Wales and current reforms to the Criminal Justice System offer an opportunity to develop an approach to offender management, rehabilitation and re-offending in Wales which is better suited in the Welsh context than are the current arrangements – and so is more likely to be effective. There are only four prisons in Wales, all of which are in the south of the country. There is little provision for juvenile and young offenders, and no prisons at all for women. All of this has far-reaching consequences for prisoners, their families and the agencies working with them. The current overcrowding of the prison estate means that the transfer of prisoners between prisons has increased, and the likelihood of Welsh prisoners being able to serve all or part of their sentences near to home is reduced. This then affects the delivery of health, education and rehabilitation services to these prisoners, and reduces the likelihood of successful resettlement on release. We believe that new prison places should be provided in north Wales, where currently none exist, and in south Wales, where there is a high demand for places for male adult offenders. We believe there should be a new approach to the treatment of female prisoners along the lines proposed by Baroness Corston in her report on vulnerable women in the prison system. This would include small, community-based residential units for female offenders offering a range of rehabilitation services, and small custodial units for those serving longer sentences. These arrangements would, we believe, address some of the considerable needs of female offenders and allow those that are primary carers (the majority) to maintain better contact with their children. In the short-term, we recommend that more support and better visiting facilities are provided for families visiting prisoners who are held long distances from home. We heard evidence of high levels of mental ill-health and self-harm amongst the Welsh prison population, particularly amongst women. Providing appropriate support services to prisoners with mental health problems and transferring prisoners with severe mental illness to secure mental health units is problematic, and more should be done to address these issues. Levels of substance misuse amongst prisoners are also high and, although there is some good work being undertaken in Wales to address this, more needs to be done to link prison and community-based services. There are some serious concerns around Welsh-language provisions for Welsh prisoners, in particular for young offenders, which could be addressed most effectively by the provision of prison places in north Wales. There is poor information on the number of Welsh-speaking prisoners, and consequently under-provision of Welsh-language materials in prisons in which they are held. Welsh-medium education should be provided for all juvenile offenders who need it, and better Welsh-language materials should be provided for adults. Providing effective education in prison is made more difficult by the rate of movement of prisoners between establishments, and by the increasing number of those serving short sentences. The transfer of information on prisoners training achievements needs to be improved in order to eliminate the unnecessary duplication of assessments. A greater consistency in the educational and training courses provided by different prisons would also make it easier for prisoners to continue their courses on transfer to another prison. More information is needed on the effectiveness of prison education for Welsh prisoners, particularly in terms of its impact on re-offending. We believe that the restorative justice programme piloted at HMP Cardiff has the potential to make a useful contribution to the support offered to victims of crime, the rehabilitation of offenders and the development of a more community-based approach to criminal justice in Wales. We welcome the developments of community courts in England and Wales and the proposal for such a court in Merthyr Tydfil, and believe that such arrangements hold some promise for a new approach to criminal justice that would fit comfortably into the Welsh context. The rehabilitation and resettlement of many Welsh prisoners is hampered by their distance from home. Losing contact with families and communities makes resettlement more difficult for prisoners, and the distances agencies are required to travel to, places a strain on their resources and restricts their scope for work. NOMS [the National Offender Management Service] should take account of these factors when allocating resources to probation and other resettlement agencies if they are to achieve the reductions in the high re-offending rate expected by the Government. Wales now has an opportunity to develop its own distinctive approach to criminal justice which better reflect the needs of Wales and which could serve as a model for development elsewhere in the UK.

The Welsh Affairs Select Committee's report is welcomed. However, it does pose the question of why these proposals were never raised 20 years ago, when the problem of Welsh prisoners became apparent. I do not think we will get the facilities to accommodate Welsh prisoners until power over the criminal justice system is devolved to Wales.

Welsh speakers have a harder time in English prisons, especially when it comes to the letters that their loved ones send to them. If they are written in the Welsh language, it can take up to a fortnight before the prisoner receives his letters because the prison has to translate them. Sometimes, prison officers will taunt prisoners and make comments that their loved ones should have written to them in English. Magazines and books in Welsh are also hard to obtain in prison because of prison policy. All Welsh literature should be allowed into the prisons without hindrance.

Another issue was raised in the Welsh press recently regarding bilingual juries. Plaid Cymru's MP Hywel Williams slammed the UK Government's stubborn refusal to press ahead with plans for bilingual juries in Wales. Citing Canada, which has bilingual juries when necessary, Mr Williams said that the decision showed the Government's lack of ambition to even try, and compared it with the forward-thinking, inclusive approach of the Welsh Assembly Government to the Welsh language.

Mr Williams laid a Private Member's Bill to this effect which, if it had been passed, would have introduced bilingual juries in Wales. But this Bill did not have UK Government support as it passed through Parliament. Hywel Williams commented:

> [The] announcement is deeply disappointing. After years of delays, the UK Government has rejected the very concept based on some rather spurious grounds. I believe that this decision was made many months ago because the Government has failed to show any real reasons why bilingual juries cannot be allowed. Meanwhile, countries such as Canada, for example, are well ahead of the UK. The Government's argument is that the introduction of a bilingual jury would remove the principle of random jury selection. What they have ignored is that there is already a language requirement – to speak English – enshrined in law. They are happy to have an exception for English but won't do it to allow Welsh speakers to be tried by their peers. This decision

is a very backwards step. Many people feel much more comfortable communicating in Welsh and, as part of the justice system, we should be allowing them every fair play to ensure a fair trial. The Government also claims that the number of Welsh speakers able to participate would be only a small percentage of the population, but, in reality, it would only be a small number of County Court cases which would require a bilingual jury. A bilingual jury would actually save money as there would be no need of translators and would be better for justice as we would hear and understand the authentic original voice of the participants. Remember that bilingual jurors would be fluent in English and Welsh, so there is nothing lost in understanding documents or parts of the case that are delivered in English. When it comes down to it, there are neither legal, practical or cost implications which would impede bilingual juries, just the bloody-mindedness of the British legal system in London...
The attitude shown here is in complete contrast with the Welsh Assembly Government where new powers are being introduced through the Welsh language measure and shows the difference in attitudes between Wales and London on these type of issues. We only have to look back to last year when the court's computer systems were unable to deal with bilingualism and sent English-only instructions throughout Wales, never mind the delay of four years since the completion of a consultation exercise to see how justice in the Welsh language is treated in London. This only goes to illustrate the need for a Welsh legal jurisdiction which would treat bilingualism as the norm, rather than some sort of peripheral exception. I shall continue to fight for this change in the courts, the one area of the Welsh language which would remain at Westminster after a successful referendum, as it shows once again that a strong Plaid Cymru voice is needed here in Westminster to fight for issues that the London parties will happily ignore.

English politicians at Westminster, on the whole, have never given a damn about Wales. We will have to wait and see if the Welsh Select Committee Report will make a blind bit of difference to Welsh prisoners and their families. It's OK talking about these matters – what is needed is positive action.

11

VETERANS IN PRISON

THERE HAVE BECOME some serious concerns about the number of ex-servicemen and women who are serving sentences throughout England and Wales. One of the first MPs to raise the issue was Elfyn Llwyd. His campaign has led to more awareness of the plight of ex-servicemen.

The National Association of Probation Officers (NAPO) produced a report in 2009 and found that 12,000 former armed service personnel were under the supervision of the Probation Service in England and Wales on either community sentences or on parole. Research by NAPO found that 8,500 veterans were in custody at any one time. Therefore, there were twice as many veterans in the criminal justice system as there were serving in military operations in Afghanistan.

The Probation Service caseload in 2008 was 243,000 including 165,000 on court order supervision and a further 47,000 on pre- or post-release from prison supervision. During the course of 2008,

205,000 persons started supervision. NAPO's survey would suggest, therefore, that at least six per cent of those currently under supervision were veterans. In 2008, 8.5 per cent of the prison population had an armed service record. Previous studies by the Home Office and Ministry of Defence found that the proportion of those in prison with a service record varied from between four and six per cent (Home Office) to 16.7 per cent (MOD). A 2007 study carried out by veterans in prison, based on prisoners self-certification, concluded that nine per cent of all inmates were veterans.

NAPO received information from staff during the summer of 2009, working in 62 different probation offices in England and Wales. In all, there were 90 case studies with regard to veterans submitted from areas throughout England and Wales.

The most common social factor among the 90 veteran cases submitted was a chronic use of alcohol, which was reported 39 times; drug misuse was reported in 13 cases. The most common conviction was for violence in a domestic setting, which occurred in 39 cases. Many believe that military service enhances the risk of domestic violence. In ten instances the offence was against a child, and there were also five serious driving offences and two convictions for burglary, one for blackmail, and one for robbery. According to NAPO staff, the number of veterans with diagnosed and undiagnosed post-traumatic stress syndrome was 24, with a further 19 veterans believed to be suffering from depression or behavioural problems. Often the symptoms did not occur until many years after active service.

The most common sentence was of a supervision order of one to three years, with a condition to attend a domestic violence programme or do unpaid work. A number of persons had a suspended sentence order and six of those on the caseload were on parole licence. Locations of active service were not provided in half the cases; however ten had served in Northern Ireland, 12 in Iraq, 11 in Afghanistan and a further seven in Bosnia.

The staff who responded to the study had between one and five veterans on their caseload. In Cheshire, 20 veterans were being supervised by 20 staff. One staff member in the south, who submitted three cases from his area, said there had been so many armed service personnel on his caseload during the last decade that he could not count them. Another in Cumbria reported having seven former soldiers on group programmes during the previous 12 months.

Few veterans reported receiving any counselling on exit from the armed services and soldiers were not routinely identified as being so at the point of arrest or when court reports were written. Had forces experience been picked up, either at arrest or report stage, it is possible that the individuals could have been referred for help and counselling, which would have affected the sentencing outcome and also their own individual prognosis.

The case histories examined showed that the majority of the ex-soldiers were suffering at some stage from post-traumatic stress disorder.

Committed staff at HMP Everthorpe have put together an advice pack for former soldiers and they offer to liaise with counselling services. But this does not appear to be available nationally, although an MoD project is planning to publish help and support for services that are available. It is also improving the awareness of welfare visits that can be arranged for ex-service prisoners. NAPO understands that the Everthorpe pack is in the process of national roll-out.

This report by NAPO into ex-servicemen and how they get treated leaves me feeling very angry. I cannot believe we treat our heroes, who have put their lives on the line for this country time and time again, in this way.

Most of our ex-servicemen are severely damaged mentally by their experiences and, unless help is available to them as soon as they come out of the army, more and more ex-servicemen are going to end up in prison.

I remember meeting an ex-serviceman called Jimmy while I was in prison and he explained to me the horrors he encountered while serving in Northern Ireland at the height of the troubles and how he ended up in prison. Jimmy told me that he was on patrol one night with his platoon when he was given orders to take his troops down the Shankill Road. Jimmy felt that something wasn't right and refused a direct order to do so. Jimmy was facing a court martial for refusing to comply with the order, and he knew this, but he had a gut feeling that something wasn't right and couldn't put a finger on it. Another platoon was sent in and sadly some of the soldiers got blown up – Jimmy's instinct was unfortunately correct. Jimmy served in Northern Ireland twice and had won a mention in dispatches on two separate occasions.

Jimmy told me how he ended up in prison. He was at a shopping precinct when he heard a loud bang and saw a man coming towards him. Jimmy said he suffered flashbacks from his time in Northern Ireland and thought this man was going to kill him so Jimmy killed him instead. Jimmy received a life sentence and, at the time, neither he nor the courts were aware that he was suffering post-traumatic stress disorder.

The last time I spoke to Jimmy he was trying to get his case reopened and, had the trial judge and his defence team known that Jimmy had PTSD, he probably wouldn't have received a life sentence but would probably have had help.

The system in relation to ex-servicemen needs to be addressed by the Government as a matter of urgency. Our men and women have suffered enough through fighting for our country: the least we can do for them is to get them the help they need. Prison is no place for our ex-servicemen and this practice of jailing our courageous heroes must be a thing of the past. A special trauma centre should be set up to help all ex-servicemen and women suffering post-traumatic stress disorder and other illnesses.

12

WHAT NEEDS TO BE DONE

* To recap, there should be a full judicial inquiry into the segregation units at prisons in England and Wales, as there is clear evidence of brutality towards prisoners.

* I'd like to see the basic, standard and enhanced regime abolished as it does not comply with the Human Rights Convention and is nothing more than a class system. The basic regime is nothing other than a segregation unit by another name which denies the basic rights of prisoners to a fair hearing.

* There should be an inquiry as to why the prison governors and the Home Office refuse to comply so that prisoners have the right of access to journalists as set out in my House of Lords judgment in July 1999. They are in contempt of court and are interfering with justice.

*   There should be a new unit set up to help ex-servicemen who come into contact with the criminal justice system, so they can be examined for post-traumatic stress disorder and given the right help and treatment rather than sent to prison.

I hope my book will bring about some serious reform of the prison system which is long overdue. I can recall prior to the 2010 general election David Cameron saying 'vote for change'. Does this extend to prisoners and the prison system? Only time will tell.

ACKNOWLEDGEMENTS

I WOULD LIKE to thank Paul Duggan for giving me the idea to write this book. I would also like to thank Liberty, Claire Dyer, Richard Ford, Vikram Dodd, John Bowen, Hugh Muir and Diana Taylor, Brian Brady and Jonathan Owen, Thomas Elin, Emyr Williams, Rosemary Bennett, Hickman & Rose Solicitors, Tony Gardner, Charles Hanson, Richard Edwards, Nigel Morris, Ben Russell, Richard Cookson, Marc Leverton, Juliet Lyon of the Prison Reform Trust, Ed Hancock, Greig Box, Justice Committee, European Commissioner Thomas Hammarberg, Andrew Norfolk and fully acknowledge your work in highlighting the issue of prisons. I thank each and every one of you.

A big thank you to Harry Fletcher of the National Association of Probation Officers for helping me with the issues of ex-servicemen in prison, and Elfyn Llwyd MP who has campaigned extensively on this issue. A big thank you to Kate Maynard and Dan Rubenstein for all the work they have done in highlighting prisoners being mistreated. Not many solicitors would challenge the authorities like you have and you are a godsend to prisoners in need.

I'd like to thank Charles Hanson for his take on prison issues which will hit a chord with many prisoners. I'd also like to thank Felix Martins, spokesperson for the Prisoners' Race Discrimination Unit, Sophie Corslet of Mind for highlighting mental health issues of prisoners, and Frances Crook from the Howard League for Penal Reform and Barnardo's, for the extensive work they do for prisoners including children in custody and many other aspects of prison issues.

A special thank you to Deborah Coles of Inquest who has helped many prisoners' families get answers as to why their loved ones have died in prison. Many thanks also go to *The Times* newspaper which has highlighted prison issues and which managed to get hold of documents that nobody else could and published them. A big thank you to the *Western Mail* and Martin Shipton. Thank you to Dr Theodore Mutale, ex-Youth Justice Board member, for highlighting children being restrained using painful techniques and the need to get rid of these practices and Sir Aynsley Green for raising similar issues.

I'd like to thank Sir Alan Beith MP, Jenny Willott MP, Dr Hywel Francis MP, Nick Herbert, Hywel Williams and David Howarth MP for highlighting prison issues in the media and raising some prison issues in a Welsh context, such as building prisons in Wales, so that prisoners can be nearer their families. Special thanks to Anne Owers who made a big difference in her role as Prisons Inspector, highlighting so many issues and making prisons safer for officers and prisoners alike: enjoy your retirement. A very special thank you to ex-officer Carol Lingard for being brave enough to speak out and highlight wrongdoing and the same to Jim Dawkins, who were both fine officers. I wish you both luck in the future.

A very, very special thank you has to go out to six serving officers: Jez Spencer and his team who have done a great job in reducing suicides in prison, Sonia

Leonard, John Hancock, Kevin Clift, Bill Hosie and Pam Chalk. These officers are a credit to the Prison Service and are a shining example how *all* prison officers should behave towards prisoners. Any prison officers who don't meet these standards should be removed from the Prison Service.

I hope my book will bring about many changes for prisoners, especially to Welsh prisoners who are isolated from their families. The fight in this regard goes on. I would like to thank Dr Michael Naughton from Bristol University, who is an inspiration and a true friend, and Gabe Tan, who is an inspiration to all those who come into contact with her – a very remarkable woman.

A very special thank you to Lynne Copson for proof-reading my book – your help has been invaluable.

A very big thank you to John Sturzaker for fighting for honest officers like Carol Lingard. Special thank you to Martin Shipton for your advice and help in preparing this book.

A special thank you has to go to my wife Claire who came up with the title of this book and is always my tower of strength. A special mention also goes to my children, who keep me going when things get tough: Kyle, Stefan, Shannon Courtney, Dainton and my granddaughter Lacy. Always in my thoughts, my son Dylan and daughter Kylie, RIP. My apologies if I've missed anyone out, there was no intention to do so.

Also from Y Lolfa:

MICHAEL O'BRIEN
with Greg Lewis

After eleven years in prison for a crime he did not commit, O'Brien reveals the truth about the CARDIFF NEWSAGENT MURDER.

y Lolfa

The DEATH of JUSTICE

£9.95

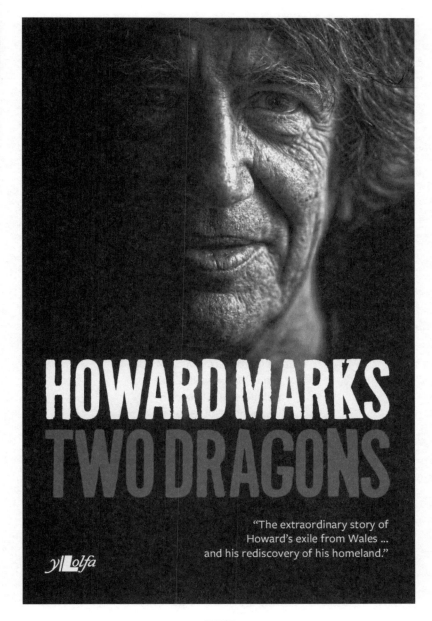

HOWARD MARKS
TWO DRAGONS

"The extraordinary story of
Howard's exile from Wales ...
and his rediscovery of his homeland."

y Lolfa

£7.95

Prisons Exposed is just one of a whole range of publications from Y Lolfa. For a full list of books currently in print, send now for your free copy of our new full-colour catalogue. Or simply surf into our website

www.ylolfa.com

for secure on-line ordering.

TALYBONT CEREDIGION CYMRU SY24 5HE
e-mail ylolfa@ylolfa.com
website www.ylolfa.com
phone (01970) 832 304
fax 832 782